No Place
Like Home

No Place Like Home

staying in, kicking back, and living it up

Michelle Kehm

Ⓟ

A PLUME BOOK

PLUME
Published by the Penguin Group
Penguin Group (USA) Inc., 375 Hudson Street, New York, New York 10014, U.S.A.
Penguin Group (Canada), 10 Alcorn Avenue,
Toronto, Ontario, Canada M4V 3B2 (a division of Pearson Penguin Canada Inc.)
Penguin Books Ltd, 80 Strand, London WC2R 0RL, England
Penguin Ireland, 25 St Stephen's Green,
Dublin 2, Ireland (a division of Penguin Books Ltd)
Penguin Group (Australia), 250 Camberwell Road,
Camberwell, Victoria 3124, Australia (a division of Pearson Australia Group Pty Ltd)
Penguin Books India Pvt Ltd, 11 Community Centre,
Panchsheel Park, New Delhi – 110 017, India
Penguin Books (NZ), Cnr Airborne and Rosedale Roads,
Albany, Auckland, New Zealand (a division of Pearson New Zealand Ltd)
Penguin Books (South Africa) (Pty) Ltd, 24 Sturdee Avenue,
Rosebank, Johannesburg 2196, South Africa

Penguin Books Ltd, Registered Offices: 80 Strand, London WC2R 0RL, England

First published by Plume, a member of Penguin Group (USA) Inc.

First Printing, March 2005
1 3 5 7 9 10 8 6 4 2

Copyright © Michelle Kehm, 2005
Illustrations copyright © Annika Wester, 2005

Ⓟ REGISTERED TRADEMARK—MARCA REGISTRADA

CIP data is available.
ISBN 0-452-28537-2

Printed in the United States of America
Set in Garamond Light
Designed by Eve L. Kirch

PUBLISHER'S NOTE
Neither the publisher nor the author is engaged in rendering professional advice or services to the individual reader. The ideas, procedures, and suggestions contained in this book are not intended as a subsitute for consulting with your physician. All matters regarding your health require medical supervision. Neither the author nor the publisher shall be liable or responsible for any loss or damage allegedly arising from any information or suggestion in this book.

The recipes contained in this book are to be followed exactly as written. The Publisher is not responsible for your specific health or allergy needs that may require medical supervision. The Publisher is not responsible for any adverse reactions to the recipes contained in this book.

To gram,
the best nester of them all

Acknowledgments

· ·

Cheers and heartfelt thanks to these exceptional people: Kelly Notaras for finding me, my editor Julie Saltman for guiding me, and my agent and friend Carolyn French for believing in me and making sure I had a warm jacket for my first New York winter. Also, thanks to my oldest and dearest friend, Stephenie Cathcart, and also Wendy, for giving me a place to nest when I had none. I heart you all.

Contents

● ●

Foreword

• •

Let's face it, ladies. Knitting needles, kitschy kitchen aprons, and home shows are taking the country by storm: nesting is back, and in a big way. But while nobody will argue that nesting is once again très today, it makes me wonder, where did it go in the first place? What happened between my grandmother's nest full of dirty dishes and diapers, sewing boxes, and buns in the oven; and my sanctuary full of bubble baths and poetry books and precious objects from my world travels? What happened to cause the act of nesting, and most domestic arts for that matter, to fall from public grace and be shunned as "women's work," even by women? And why have they now resurfaced, stronger than ever?

The key to answering that question rests in the term "women's work." Somewhere down the line, the work that women do was billed as being less important than the work of men. Who started this rumor and why really isn't the issue at hand here—the issue is that women actually bought into it. With the feminist movements of the '60s and '70s, domestic duties such as cooking, sewing, and creating a fun, fabulous place to live lost their value to "men's" jobs such as doctoring and lawyering; and suddenly, every self-respecting woman believed that spending her days at home meant she was, in effect, wasting her life. This thought process may seem extreme, and it was. In effect, it dismissed women and the work they had traditionally done for centuries. But on the upside, this new yearning for equality drove packs of women out of their nests and into college classrooms and corporate offices, which ultimately paved the road to economic freedom for their daughters and their daughters' daughters.

This is where nesting comes full circle. Where once women felt obligated to perform certain tasks either because it was all they were taught or they were financially dependent, today's generation of nesters have been intellectually and economically liberated. Nesting is now our choice. It is no longer seen as dull and limiting, but instead as creative, and ironically enough, liberating. We bake bread, knit afghans, rearrange furniture, arrange flowers, and stay in because we straight-up enjoy it. So here we are again, ladies, right back where we started—in the home. But this time, the sistas are doin' it for themselves.

Introduction

●●●●●●●●●●●●●●●●●●●●●●●●●●●●●●●●●●●●

What is nesting, exactly?

Nesting is claiming your own private space and making it your own. It's about getting comfortable, burrowing in, and most importantly—staying in. While much of nesting is about painting a wall red, slipcovering a sofa, or hanging café curtains, it's just as much about staying in on a rainy Sunday, taking a hot bath, doing laundry, and having friends over. Nesting is about doing anything you want in the privacy of your own nest space—as long as you do it for you.

Yes, nesting has come a long way, baby—and what a long, strange trip it's been. As women, we no longer have to rely on the boys to bring home the bacon—we've learned to raise the whole hog. We answer to ourselves, indulge ourselves, and love ourselves. We're picky about partners, and many of us make more money than our partners. The term "spinster" has gone the way of the one-hit wonder—sugar daddies are out, independent women are in.

In light of this newly proclaimed feminist domesticity, the nesting chicks of today have opportunities that Samantha Stevens and Carol Brady never even dreamed of. We have the opportunity to find, fill, and fluff our very own, very special nests. Maybe that means we paint everything pink and gold and hang Shiva posters on the walls; or maybe we match our preppy chambray pillows perfectly to our bed shams. Maybe we deck out our nest in stainless steel and modern minimalist; or we paint our living room black and have a make-out session on a leopard-print love seat we re-covered ourselves. The point is, we can turn a spare room into a yoga studio, a hip home office, a chill lounge, or a bootie-full baby's room. We can surround ourselves with all the colors, ideas, objects, and people we love, and we really can make a place all our own. Nesting is not about creating the perfect space for your man to lounge and kick off his Pumas in; it's about creating the perfect space for you. How deliciously selfish!

But let us take a moment to thank our beloved mothers, and their mothers, and their mothers. It is they who pioneered the road for us, who sacrificed and struggled and vacuumed and valiumed away the days of their lives while building a better, more independent future for their daughters. Without their endurance, patience, and guidance, we might still be dusting in heels.

So get your paintbrushes, scissors, knitting needles, and mixing bowls ready. Let's reclaim this new dawn of domesticity and make it our own. Read on, and learn how to make your home, studio, apartment, or bedroom into a perfectly personalized nest. On the cheap.

PART ONE

· ·

Find, Fill & Feather

More than a feeling: After ending a relationship with a wonderful boy I had been living with for four years, I suddenly found myself heartbroken—and homeless. I moved in with a couple of good friends for what was to be a couple of weeks but ended up being a couple of years, on and off. I went from sleeping on the couch to moving my bedroom set into the spare room. Living with friends was incredibly comforting to me, but there was also something about the house itself that made me want to stay. That house had a great feeling—a very special vibe. Alas, when it came time for me to move out and find a space to call my own, I knew I wanted a place where I felt that same good energy. I hit the streets and looked at apartments for three weeks but found nothing that grabbed me. I was comparing everything to my friends' ever-so-nesty space. Then I realized that the special feeling I was searching for wasn't something that's just found—it's something that's created. This is what nesting is all about—creating your own special space. No matter if you're living in a New York studio, a Tennessee Tudor home, or your parents' basement, it's all about filling a space with your own good mojo.

Find Your Nest

∙ ∙

Let's get nesty!

Ever see the bodacious Jane Fonda in the 1968 film *Barbarella*? She's the perfect example of a gal getting it on with her nesting talents. Her job as an intergalactic bad girl demanded she float around in a spaceship, yet she managed to create the foxiest, baddest love nest/home office in the galaxy—not to mention looking fabulous while lounging in it. Her wall-to-wall-to-wall orange shag carpet alone makes renting the DVD well worth it.

The point? If Barbarella can make a cramped space-can look oh-so-fabulous, you too can give any place your own uniquely funky, sugary, buttoned-up, or bad-girl touch, and make it your own. But first things first, ladies. Before you can create the perfect nest, you have to find the space; and unlike Barbarella, you have so many options it can make your ponytails spin. Do you want an apartment, house, or house share? Do you want to live in the city, in the burbs, in an industrial area? Do you want your own place or roommates? Yard or no yard? Quiet or crazy?

Whether you're buying in the city or renting in the sticks, moving out of your mama's house for the first time or moving for the fifth time this year, narrowing down what you want will ultimately help you get it. So to assist in your perfect nest quest, here is a fun quiz to help you nail down what type of nesting situation is best for you, plus a few things to ponder before you plop down that application fee.

The nest test

Ready to find a place and start nesting? Before you hit the pavement for a week or three of blisterous heel work, take this quick and easy nest test. It will help you hone your search and get what you want. Remember, darlin', it's all in the details.

Your ideal social situation is:

   a. Crowded bar, sweating on the dance floor
   b. Quiet café enjoying jazz, wheat-free scones, and herbal infusions
   c. Starbucks, your iBook, a caramel Frappuccino
   d. A Vietnamese restaurant where nobody speaks English
   e. Alone

Your day job is:

   a. In the heart of a mega-metropolis
   b. In a walkable, busable, or bikable neighborhood
   c. On a corporate campus outside the city
   d. In your home office
   e. Working only when you have to

Your preferred way to get around is:

   a. Your own two feet
   b. Your bike

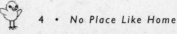

    c. Your car
    d. Public bus/subway/light rail/monorail
    e. Your broom

You spend your weeknights:

    a. Trying the hippest new restaurants
    b. Visiting friends
    c. Helping your mom do the dishes
    d. Reading Sylvia Plath
    e. Chopping firewood

And your weekends:

    a. Club hopping until 4 a.m.
    b. Trying new microbrews at the local pub
    c. Getting your nails filled and prowling the mall
    d. Antiquing and thrift store shopping
    e. Meditating in the mountains

If you answered mostly a: You're a city gal. You work, play, and prowl in the city. You know all the top spots, all the hipsters, and where the action is. You feel at home among the skyscrapers, taxis, and late-night diners—you want to nest in the city you so adore.

If you answered mostly b: You're the girl next door. You like the thrill of the city but enjoy getting away from it all when you go home. You cherish your local restaurants, your community grocery store, your neighborhood café, your neighbors. Find yourself a funky, charming neighborhood just outside the city.

If you answered mostly c: You're a suburban girl. You've got a nice car, a ruthless mall-shopping strategy, a set of French-tipped nails to die for, and a best friend in your mom. The burbs are in your blood. Find a nice place with new carpeting and a covered garage that's close to the fam and friends.

If you answered mostly d: You're an indie girl. You crave diversity, quality, creativity, and anything but normalcy. You may even be an aspiring artist. Find yourself a place in a cool, artsy neighborhood—or maybe the city's international district.

If you answered mostly e: You're a nature girl. You like things quiet, simple. You feel good about yourself and don't need the chaos of the city and its party scene. You're a lucky one. You can live just about anywhere because you create your own environment. But you may want to shy away from the inner city.

DTC (Deciphering those classifieds)

DW (dishwasher): Your manicure will last and last
NP (no pets): Hide your cat when the landlord comes a knockin'
NS/ND (no smoking/no drugs): Icksnay on the par-tay
+ UTIL (plus utilities): Put a little aside each month for utilities on top of rent
W/D (washer and dryer): No more scrounging for quarters!
Cozy: It's a tissue box
Cute: See cozy
Fee: Pay me for finding this place for you
Fixer-upper: Blood, sweat, and tears required
Great location: Good go-out, take-out, and hang-out spots
Interesting neighborhood: Bars on the windows
Mini kitchen: Can you live without four stove burners, an oven, and a standard-size refrigerator?
Railroad-style: Someone has to walk through your room to get to the toilet
Shared duties: Welcome to boot camp
Vegan: Don't even think of frying up that bacon in a pan

Nest etc.

Safe-T girl

When you find a place you like, think about if you'll feel safe there. Are the bushes cut back, or are there ample places somebody could hide? Will you have a long walk from the car, bus, or subway to your door? Is there a scary back alley? Does the building have a security system? Are the neighbors picky about who they buzz in to the building? Check the doors, make sure they're solid, not cheap and hollow, and make sure that they have working dead bolts. Check the locks on the windows. If you're looking at apartments, you might want to get a unit up off street level. Go back at night and see what it's like after dark— would you feel safe walking home in the wee hours?

Go eco

If you're planning on renting a place built before 1978, it probably has paint that contains lead, which can cause serious health problems, especially if you plan on doing any sanding, have a child, or want to have one soon. Contact the EPA's (Environmental Protection Agency) lead information center at 1-800-532-3394 for more information.

Fuzzy buddies

Pet interviews are all the craze these days. Even if a place allows pets, the landlord may still want to interview you and your four-legged friend to make sure he or she's not going to chew up the place. Please take your pet's feelings into consideration when you're looking for a nest. Your bull mastiff's not going to enjoy being cooped up in a SoHo studio all day, nor is your skittish kitten going to like living in a triplex that's ruled by rottweilers.

Mo' money, mo' money

On top of first month's rent, last month's rent, and a security deposit in advance, you may also have to pay an application fee. Unscrupulous property managers sometimes try to make extra cash with these application fees by accepting as many applications as possible. Be smart. You may not want to fork over the cash if there are already ten people in front of you waiting to get in.

Tips

- The best time to start perusing the Sunday classifieds is the first half of each month. Tenants generally have until the tenth of the month to give landlords notice that they're moving out, but you may not be able to move in until the beginning of the following month. The landlord may want to paint, clean, and prep for you!

- Sometimes the hottest properties aren't found in the paper. For the freshest rentals on the block, online listings change every day, and sometimes every hour. Do an online search for rental listings in your area.

- Imagine: you fall in love with a one-bedroom with a stainless steel fridge, gas stove, and washer and dryer, only to find out upon move-in that the appliances belonged to the last tenant and moved to Ohio along with them. Always ask which appliances come with the place.

- Before you sign a rental lease, ask your landlord what the penalties are for breaking the contract, just in case you decide to become a surf bum or live in London for the summer.

- If you're a pack rat, shoe fetishist, or avid thrifter, think about where you can stash your stuff. Houses are usually better for storage, as they have attics and basements, but apartments may have community storage space. Ask about it.

- In large cities like New York, using a broker to help you find an apartment is expensive, but they often have the inside scoop on the best digs. If you have a job that pays a decent dollar, it might be worth it.

- Scouting out the perfect place is just like looking for the perfect outfit for the biggest party of the year. Take a friend who's brutally honest. He or she may pick up on things you don't, like the beautiful mosaic tile work in the bath, the smelly Dumpsters in the back alley, or the cutie who lives next door.

Color Your Nest

● ●

I was sixteen years old the first time I painted the interior of a house. My dad was selling his early 1900s bungalow in Portland, Oregon, and he said he'd pay me and my friends $35 apiece to paint the place before he put it on the market. He wanted us to fill in the nail holes, paint over the grease marks splashed on the kitchen walls, and hide the mildew spots in his *Purple Rain* purple (it was the '80s, mind you) bathroom. So one Saturday, me and two of my best friends donned our Lawman dungarees, threw the boom box, Duran Duran cassettes, paint buckets, and brushes into the trunk of my VW Rabbit, and made a day of it over at Dad's. He wasn't there while we were painting, and the three of us smoked cigarettes and laughed the day away. When we were finished, the walls looked good as new, the bathroom was white, and we had lots of great stories to tell. Like how Anne fell against a wet wall and skunked her whole back, how Stephanie found a gold mine of beer bottles (10¢ refund each!) in the basement, and how my dad (who claimed the beer bottles were there when he bought the place) pulled a surprise visit and made a beeline for the exact kitchen cupboard where we had stashed our Marlboros. Busted.

Paintbrush, anyone?

Painting is perhaps the fastest, easiest, and cheapest way to make a new space your own. A coat of fresh color can open up the small spaces, cozy up the cold places, highlight cool features like moldings and built-in shelving, and hide ugly features like archaic radiators.

If you find the perfect little apartment but the living room is lemon yellow and the bedroom Barbie pink, don't sweat it. A bad paint job is like a bad dye job—it's only temporary. Even if the place has a fresh coat of clean white paint, your new walls are but an opportunity to express yourself and start building your nest with customized colors, textures, and patterns.

Color mojo

Never underestimate the power of color. Color is what makes a pink sweater so yummy, a set of baby blues so dreamy, and a room either a place to hang in or run from. Color has the ability to welcome or refuse, lull or caffeinate, arouse or deflate, and its effects are both emotional and physical. On the emotional level, a rich, deep saffron might warm and intrigue us, a cubicle gray might bore and depress us, and a bright orange might make us want to jump up and juice something. On the physical level, a room painted a light color will appear larger, a room painted dark will seem smaller, and a ceiling painted white will look higher than a ceiling painted midnight blue.

Yes, color is witchy, and you'll want to put some thought into choosing the ones you're going to surround yourself with for the next year or so. Walk around your place and think about what you want to say with color. Think about what each room will be used for, what feeling and moods you want each room to evoke. Look at the size of the rooms: Do you want to open a room up with light colors, or make it appear more intimate with warmer ones? Do you already have a sofa, lots of artwork, and a beautiful bedcover from Morocco? Take their coloring into consideration. Then think of your entire place as one. Will the rooms' colors work together to give your place a unified theme?

If this is too much to chew on, no worries. Here are some basic color rules from the pros to start you off on the right track. And if this is still too much to digest, here's an inside secret: just choose the colors you're naturally drawn to. Look in your closet and see what colors you buy the most. Take your fave dresses, sweaters, and pants, throw them out on the bed, and put together outfits. Then take the colors in those outfits and create the color themes for your new nest.

And remember, if you do paint your boudoir a color that's way too punk or priss, all you have to do is paint over it. Problem solved.

Color horoscopes

Colors can be divided into three main groups: those that stimulate and uplift, those that relax and calm, and those that provide harmony and balance. Knowing about the power of color can help you make selections that will give you and your new nest good mojo. Remember though, these are basic generalizations—when it comes to how a color will really make you feel, every hue is different. My point? There's pink, and then there's fuchsia.

Red: Red is the color of blood and danger, love and anger, fire and creation. Like a bad breakup, it refuses to be ignored and stimulates strong emotions. In a nutshell, red is strength. Red will warm you, excite you, and heighten your motivations—perfect for setting the mood behind the love seat, and in the hallway on the way to the bedroom.

Pink: I find it interesting that you can take all the furious glory of red, add a little white, and you're left with the color that symbolizes softness and frailty. I don't know how I feel about pink. Some girls love it, some girls hate it, but one thing's for sure: it denotes delicacy and can be delicious slathered in the kitchen or dining area.

Orange: Orange is a warm yet daring color that causes an increase in heart rate and encourages us to be bold. Orange conveys creativity and uniqueness, and while it can be obnoxious when in its life-jacket hue, add a little white and you have peach in all its freshness and health; add a little brown and you have spicy pumpkin. Play with it.

Yellow: Yellow is the most reflective and bright color. It stimulates the brain, welcomes light, calms, and is cheery in main social areas—but only when toned down or warmed up from its glaring bumble-bee self. Think a comfortable cozy saffron, a warm toasted wheat, or a lavishly creamy butter. The trick to yellow is finding a shade that keeps attention, rather than screams for it.

Green: Green is natural, relaxing, and easy on the eyes. Soft sages and celadons are popular because they are so relaxing and light; darker greens tend to be stagnant and can suffocate a room if painted on too thick. Green is also believed to aid digestion, so it can wear well in dining areas, but beware of yellow greens, as they quickly turn sickly.

Blue: Blue is soothing and contemplative. Use blue in living areas where you want to inspire conversation, and in the bathroom to relax and honor the properties of water. Navy blue is dependable, sky blue is meditative, sea blue is restorative. Be wary of blue in the kitchen, as it's known to make people lose their appetites.

Purple: Purple is a powerful color long associated with luxury, royalty, and The Artist Formerly Known as Prince. Purple is beautiful as a colorwash, and lilac and lavender evoke serenity and calm. But as purple doesn't appear often in nature, too much of it can seem artificial.

Brown: Brown inspires feeling of home and hearth, of wood and forest, of food and earth. Brown itself can be a bit drab and dark, but when spiced up with warm reds or saffrons, it can be quite lovely. Beware of beige. Beige is neither natural nor reassuring—it's just plain awful.

Gray: Gray represents conservatism, traditionalism, and corporatism, but it does have its perks. If you offset a gray wall with the right accents, say red or orange, it can be quite nice. Warm up gray's cold side by trimming with red and yellow; cool it down with green and blue.

White: White symbolizes purity, peace, and cleanliness, and it always works in small doses. If you really want to live on the edge, think about using a variation of white. A bluish white might evoke a contemplative edge, a linen white may say prep, a yellowish white may warm up a room like a pearl. The only downside of white is that too much of it can seem sterile (like a hospital) and cheap (like a disposable foam cup).

Black: Black is sexy. Black is sophisticated. But it's a hard color to pull off with paint—it literally sucks the light out of a room. It can look elegant and sleek as a decorative and trim paint, maybe on a banister, windowsill, or floor molding. Try painting some chairs, or a table, or bookshelf black instead of an entire wall. Or what the heck, paint it all black. It's your place.

Room-by-room color

Now that you know a little about the power of color, here are some suggestions for harnessing this power, room by room.

Dining Room: The space where we eat, drink, and be merry. Reds are known to speed up metabolism, and orange affects how we communicate with others. Play with these two colors to create rich reds and golden oranges that will stimulate warmth and goodwill.

Living Room: The space we lounge in, relax in, entertain in. Sea blues and greens promote relaxation, and blue can also be a conversation enhancer. Warm up the cool, sedating effect of green with the heartbeat of red, which is its complementary color. If you want your living room to have a dramatic, intimate personality, drape it in sensuous jewel colors.

Kitchen: Cooking is a creative process, and nothing beats oranges, peaches, and golden yellows to inspire the cook and bring warmth into a room. Warm pinks and plums are also yummy and do well in the food room.

Bathroom: The room where we cleanse, heal, and rejuvenate ourselves. Water is the main element of the bath, and Mediterranean blues, aquamarines, and turquoises are lovely. To warm up a too-cool blue, add touches of coral, golden yellow, and peach with painted trim or accessories.

Bedroom: The room where we relax, sleep, and get it on. It's also where we spend one-third of our lives, so have your boudoir your way. For all of you love kittens, reds and oranges stimulate sexual

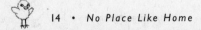

activity; all of you too-busy bees, soft greens, peaches, lilacs, and lavenders evoke a sense of calm.

Color cheat sheet

Still tearing your hair out over color? Chill, and check out these complementary colors. Anyone who's anyone in interior design uses these color combos because they always enhance each other. Different shades will create different results, but keep playing and eventually you'll get something that works.

Blue & orange	Red-violet & yellow-green
Yellow & violet	Blue-violet & yellow-orange
Red & green	Red-orange & blue-green

Top ten color tips

1. Start with what you already have. Look at your furnishings, your artwork, your curtains, and then select wall colors that complement those colors.

2. A good color scheme is always a balancing act. If you have an orange accent wall in one room, balance that out with its complementary color—a blue accent wall in another room.

3. Don't match your green walls perfectly to your green rug perfectly to your green lamp. Make the colors just a bit off—this creates interest.

4. Want a room to be soothing? Pick colors with similar values. Put two colors next to each other, squint, and if the colors kind of bleed into each other, they have a similar value.

5. Want a room to scream? Pick one bold color, then paint the trim a contrast color like white or black.

6. Cool tones add light and space and can make a room look less cluttered. Warm tones bring things together. A room painted red can actually be set at a lower temperature than a room painted a cool blue!

7. When you find a color chip you like at the paint store, go one shade lighter as color intensifies once it inhabits a large space.

8. Try the color on for size. Buy a sample quart, paint an old board, and move it around the room to see how the color gets on with your furniture, rug, and accessories.

9. Don't skimp on the goods. The right paint will make your walls look creamy, alive, and vibrant. The right brushes and rollers will save you time and energy, and help you avoid paint drips on the floor.

10. A six-pack of good beer will make your friends happy at the end of a long, messy day of painting.

Go eco: Safe synthetic and natural paints

Both oil and latex paints are petroleum products, pumped full of hundreds of ozone-depleting and carcinogenic chemicals that slowly release into the environment and never biodegrade.

Thank goodness there are alternatives.

Low-toxin synthetic paints are the easiest safe paints to get your hands on. Brands like AFM/Safecoat (www.afmsafecoat.com), Bioshield Paint (www.bioshieldpaint.com), and Rodda Paint's Horizon line (www.roddapaint.com) are readily available; and while not 100 percent natural, they generally contain far fewer toxic chemicals than latex and oil paints and are suitable for chemically sensitive folks.

Although a bit more difficult to find, natural paints are the real deal when it comes to eco-friendliness. They are made from delicious ingredients such as milk proteins, lanolin, and beeswax; their coloring pigments come from earth, minerals, and plants. Contrary to popular belief, natural paints are not that expensive, it's just that many have to be ordered online and then shipped from Europe, which adds to cost. But with all the Hollywood celebs and organic folks demanding natural paints nowadays, things are changing fast. Aglaia Natural Paints from Germany (www.aglaiapaint.com) are now available in the United States. The colors are rich, and the paint itself smells like an Aveda sa-

lon. Delicious all around! Get online and search "natural paint" to find out more. Ain't nothing like the real thing, baby.

How many gallons?

It's best to do an estimate of how many gallons of paint you'll need (especially if you're custom-color mixing, as it's usually not returnable). Most paint manufacturers list coverage on the container, and it's usually estimated in square feet.

Square feet = length of a wall x height of a wall

Measure and add the separate lengths of all the walls in a room, and multiply it by the height of one wall (all walls should be the same height). If you plan on painting the ceiling, just multiply the room length by the room width and add this to your overall figure. You'll also need to make adjustments for the windows and doors. If you're tired of the math, the standard door deduction is twenty square feet; the standard window is fifteen square feet.

Always estimate higher rather than lower. The leftover paint will invariably come in handy for touch-ups after a dinner-party-turned-food-fight.

Paint par-tay

Of course you'd rather hang with your friends than spend time prepping for painting, but down, girl. A bit of prep work is necessary in order to ensure the fabulous results you deserve. Here's a ten-step process to make prepping as quick and pleasant as possible.

Paint prep

1. Undress your walls. Take down your velvet Elvis paintings, mirrors, and all your Joan Jett posters. All of them.
2. Remove outlet covers. Turn off the power first!

3. **Elbow room.** Move furniture into the center of the room, and cover with a plastic drop cloth or old sheet to protect from paint splatters.

4. **Repair.** Small dings and nail holes magically disappear with a little something called spackling compound, available at hardware stores.

5. **Scrape.** If you have ugly paint bubbles or alligator-skin paint, scrape it off. Manual paint scrapers are available at hardware stores.

6. **Sand.** Give all surfaces a light sanding to help your new paint adhere to the old.

7. **Clean.** Go over all surfaces with a mild cleaner like Simple Green, or see page 29 for natural cleaners you can make yourself!

8. **Tape.** Tape anywhere you don't want paint to reach—blue

painter's tape is best and available at hardware stores. Go over tape edges with a putty knife to seal them tight.

9. Drop cloth. Plastic drop cloths are cheap and disposable, but be careful as they're slippery. You can also tape down sheets or newspaper.

10. Party favors. Find a good painting outfit (be functional, this is not the time to be fashionable). Tie your hair up. Set your music up so you won't have to play DJ with paint-covered hands. Put pizza delivery on speed dial. Get a wet rag(s) for your hands and the paint drips that are sure to come. Get all of the friends you were able to bribe into one room, and make a day of it. Have fun!

Tasty tricks

Ladies, let the fun begin! It's time to make your nest into a space you'll love and all your friends will secretly envy. Imagine one red wall that glows golden from within; an asymmetrical pattern of pearly blue diamonds behind your sofa; or your bed framed by a fabulous, Asian-style headboard painted directly on the wall. With a little patience, luck, and know-how, it can all be yours.

Following are a few tricks to get the creative juices flowing, but if you're really serious about tricking out your nest, go to the library or just hop online and search for painting techniques. You'll find more detailed information on the ideas listed below, plus a slew of other DIY (do-it-yourself) painting tricks to boot! Most importantly, don't let the idea of getting artistic intimidate you. When it comes to many of these techniques, the most important ingredient is your imagination. Express yourself!

Colorwashing

In colorwashing, either a diluted paint or a colorwash glaze (a translucent paint) is applied layer upon layer, so that in the end subtle gradations of color show through. The effect is a rich, multifaceted finish that light travels through rather than bounces off of.

> **Tip**
>
> The pigments in natural colorwash glazes blend the most beautifully, but if you're going to use a synthetic glaze, one that contains oil will dry slower and allow you more time to play with effects.

A rule of thumb for colorwashing is that you start with one or two solid base coats of a white or color, then apply thin layers of colorwash glaze, slowly adding, diffusing, or changing the color (like how yellow over pink creates a juicy peach). A good colorwash relies on blending glazes while they're still wet, so you might want to buddy up for the project: two hands work faster than one.

Brushes, rags, sponges, and even crumpled-up paper all create fabulous texture. The key is to work your tool of choice in circular motions to feather out any hard marks. Try applying several different glaze colors on the tool at once for ultra-dreamy color depth. For vertical texture, drag a stiff, dry, long-haired brush over a coat of wet glaze, starting at the ceiling and ending at the floor, exposing the previous layer of color in long, grassy lines. This effect also works well with a wide-tooth comb or custom-cut window squeegee. Or apply the glaze using a roller with a funky textured sleeve, or go over a wet glaze with a clean, dry roller for just a touch of texture.

Wall to-dos

Accent wall: If you want to introduce a strong color like red, orange, or black into your nest, think about painting just one wall that color. Make the one accent wall a darker color than the other three, and repeat the color throughout the room with accessories to balance it all out.

Waistlining: A waistline is when you divide a wall into two parts horizontally and paint the bottom one color, the top another. I've done this in my living room with the lower part of the wall painted a desert sand and the top part plus the ceiling a sky blue—the effect is lovely. Don't divide the room exactly in half, though. Throw the proportions off just a bit to create asymmetrical interest.

Stencils: Stenciled designs look fabulous around doorways, windows, in corners; or run a bracelet line of flames or flowers across a wall. Stencil books abound in arts and craft stores, or you can make your own. Trace any image onto Mylar or other stiff material, then cut it out with a utility knife.

Stamping: When I was a kid, I couldn't turn in a single piece of homework without stamping flowers, stars, and butterflies all over it. This same stamping vigor can look fab on your walls. Premade stamps are available at arts and craft stores. You can also make your own stamps by tracing (or freehanding) a design on foam, cutting out the foam, and gluing it onto a wood block.

Stars, stripes, and diamonds: Low on artwork? Nothing fills an empty wall better than easy-to-paint geometric designs. Imagine a pearly pink-and-gray argyle pattern behind the sofa, thick vertical stripes stretching your walls to the heavens, or any funky geometric combination your brilliant mind can conjure up. Unless you want the design to be the room's main event, keep the colors subtle. A nice effect is to use the same colors, but in different finishes: say super-glossy lilac stripes painted over a flat, matte lilac base.

Freehand: What better place to display your drawing talents than the walls of your very own nest? Always draw the design first with light pencil, charcoal, or chalk; and then use an artist's quality brush to fill it in with paint. Use freehand details to personalize stenciled and stamped designs, too.

DIY wallpaper

If you have any aspirations whatsoever to use conventional wallpaper on your walls, let me just ask you one thing—are you mad? Wallpapering is a big, sticky, stinky mess—unless it's this fresh, do-it-yourself wallpaper, of course! It's a super way to customize and add unique flair to any room in your nest. Make it, then glue it on an accent wall in the living room, the inside of your coat closet, or the entire bathroom!

Find an image you like; it could be a line drawing of a dragonfly, a Chinese character, or a picture of Mick Jagger's lips. Take the image down to Kinko's and blow it up. When you get the image looking just as you like it, make enough copies to cover an entire wall, plus a few extra, then trim them down to a square using a big paper cutter.

Take the stack home and make a pot of tea, the stronger the better. Pour yourself a cup first, and then, using a brush or a sponge, use the rest to tint the paper copies. Tea is a natural dye and will give your images a weathered, antiqued look. Play with different teas to find a color you like—green tea will look different than mango-ginger will look different than Earl Grey—or use a colorwash glaze or your kid sister's watercolor kit. You just want to add color without covering the image underneath. Dye your images, and once they're bone-dry, glue them to the wall using wallpaper glue; or if you're chemically sensitive, a flour and water mixture will work, but add a tablespoon of boric acid to chase mold away.

Have fun with how you display your images. Butt them up against each other, alternate different images, alternate colors—experiment! Once your images are up and looking gorgeous, let everything dry completely, and then go over it all with two coats of a clear, water-based lacquer to seal. Presto! One-of-a-kind wallpaper! You can also use old love letters, Xeroxed photos, or sheet music; or use it to line cupboards instead of as wallpaper. Just use your imagination.

Fancy Your Floors

······································

Y ou can have the hippest crib with the most chi-chi furnishings, but if your carpet smells like cat pee, it's all over. Always take the condition of the floors into consideration before signing a lease. If a floor is stained or smells, you are perfectly justified in asking the landlord to clean, replace, or refinish the carpet or hardwoods before you move in. But for those of you who found floors you fancy and want to keep them in tip-top condition, this one's for you.

Quickie carpet cosmetics

Odors: If your place still smells like the salmon puffs you cooked two weeks ago, first try a sprinkle-on, vacuum-up carpet deodorizer (see page 29 for a delicious aromatherapeutic recipe). You can also try a spray-on odor neutralizer (see the scented vinegar recipe on page 29.)

Dirt: For an entryway or other particularly dirty spot, try a foam-on, vacuum-up product, and put down a rug if it's a high-traffic spot. For an overall drab shag, however, you'll want to do a deep clean. Rent yourself a carpet cleaner from a home center or supermarket and get to it.

Burns: If a burn (or any stain) is just on the surface, take a nail clipper or small scissors and clip off the tops of the burned fibers. If the burn is deep, you may want to operate. Cut out the burn in a small, square slice. Then find a spare piece of the same carpet, cut a replacement patch to size, and use double-stick carpet tape to stick it in place.

Candle wax: When your candle runneth over, grab an ice pack and freeze the wax solid. Then take nail clippers or small scissors and see if you can cut off the waxy tops of the fibers. If there's still wax left, take a paper towel, lay it over the wax, and go over it with the tip of a hot iron. The paper towel will absorb the hot wax.

Nail polish: While the polish is still wet, lightly place a paper towel over it, absorb as much as possible, then break out the nail polish remover and blot. Repeat. If the polish has dried, see if you can scrape any of it off using a spoon or any blunt edge, and then try cutting off the tops of the stained fibers.

Cleaning your hardwoods

Before you do anything to your wood floors, you need to determine what kind of finish you have. Take a white rag, dip it in mineral spirits, and rub at a small area of your floor off in the corner somewhere. If an orangy residue comes off on the rag, you have a wax finish. Most wood floors installed before 1970 were finished with wax. If nothing comes off on the rag, you've got yourself a hard finish.

For a wax finish, go over the floor with a lightly dampened, soft towel (try taking an old push broom and wrapping the towel around the end of it.) Don't get the towel too wet, water and wood don't mix! Do small sections at a time, immediately wiping the dampened area with a soft, dry rag. Many professionals advise against using soap of any kind on wood floors, even Murphy Oil Soap. They say it only leaves a residue.

If you have a hard finish floor, first try the wax finish method detailed above. If your floor is still dirty or sticky, try a solution of 1 cup white vinegar to 1 gallon lukewarm water, again drying the floor immediately. Never use vinegar on a wax floor, as vinegar eats wax.

Clean Start

To me, cleaning is kind of like cooking. I love it, as long as some-body's not making me do it. As for cleaning, I hated it when I lived with two guys and was the only one who cared that the bath-room walls were growing a new strain of mold. But when I moved into a situation where everyone pulled their own weight (an all-girl situation, mind you), I rediscovered the therapeutic properties of clean-ing. I came down with some pretty bad cases of writer's block while working on this book, and when my mind would hit a dead end, sometimes I'd crank up the Bjork, get a bucket of suds, and wash something. The music, warm water, and clean smell of the soap did more than clean away the dirt, it cleaned the cobwebs from my mind.

Do it for you

Housecleaning has a bad rap, but, ladies, you have to remember that when you're building your nest, everything you do, you do it for you. So get over your cleaning aversions already, invest in a good pair of rubber gloves, and get down to work. Before you start filling your nest, you want to give it a good scrubbing and clean it of the old tenant's smells, hairballs, and dust bunnies. You'll at least want to wipe out kitchen cupboards and drawers, clean the tub and toilet, and give your floors a nice, clean sweep.

Clean green

Before you stock up on products for your cleaning spree, think about what's in them. Ammonia, bleach, phosphoric and sulfuric acids? These ingredients are considered hazardous waste, so why would you spray them on your kitchen counter, floors, and bathtub?

Conventional cleaners not only cost you—they cost the environment. Thank goodness plenty of effective, biodegradable and phosphate-free cleaning products are popping up these days. Earth Friendly Products (www.ecos.com), Planet (www.planetinc.com), and Seventh Generation (www.seventhgen.com) offer an array of eco-cleaning solutions; find them at natural food stores. While these may not be much easier on your pocketbook, they are easier on the planet. But if you're serious about saving both money and the environment, why not make your own cleaning products? All you need are a few basic ingredients, some scrumptious essential oils (see below), and to turn the page. You'll be pleased with the cheap and squeaky-clean results; plus they smell naturally delicious!

Aroma-clean

Some essential oils actually have cleaning and disinfecting properties for a power-packed, aroma-cleaning experience. Please note that in order for the oil's cleaning (and healing) properties to work, you have to use a therapeutic-grade essential oil, not a cheap synthetic oil. You can buy real oils at natural food stores or online (www .adhumanitas.com and www.youngliving.com are good). Here are a few of my favorite oils in terms of scent and cleaning properties.

Lemon, orange, grapefruit, lime: These uplifting, antibacterial citrus oils take grease out of your way.

Lavender: An all-around disinfectant that makes even cleaning the toilet a euphoric experience.

Eucalyptus: Got a cold? Eucalyptus eases congestion while disinfecting your germy bathroom.

Pine: Pine's powerful punch includes degreasing, disinfecting, and keeping your mind sharp to boot!

Tea tree: After somebody's been sick, spread this oil around to fight bacteria, fungus, and viruses.

Peppermint: Disinfects and gets your nest minty fresh!

I was first introduced to these eco-cleaning wonders in Karen Logan's book, *Clean House, Clean Planet*. It's a great resource if you're into using natural products to clean anything and everything, or if you want to make homemade, eco-friendly gifts.

Baking soda and essential oil

Baking soda cleans, softens water, neutralizes odors, and deodorizes—just add your favorite essential oil for a cheap, effective, aroma-cleaning experience!

Make me: Pour a box of Arm & Hammer baking soda into a mixing bowl, and drop by drop, use a fork to stir in a therapeutic-grade essential oil, being careful not to scent it too strongly. Put the soda in a shaker of some sort—a cleaned-out parmesan cheese shaker works great.

Use me: Sprinkle on to clean just about anything: greasy pots and pans, stovetops, countertops, sinks, tubs, microwaves, toilet bowls. For extra-tough stains, add 1 to 2 tablespoons of fresh lemon juice, soak, and scrub as necessary. Pour it down drains and let it sit for a cleansing fresher-upper; sprinkle it at the bottom of your garbage can; put it under sinks and in refrigerators to deodorize. Make your whole nest smell like a spa by sprinkling the mixture on your carpet, letting it sit overnight, and vacuuming up in the morning. A great incense alternative for smoke-sensitive folk! A little goes a long way, so use sparingly, and if you're left with a gritty residue after cleaning, just spray on some scented white vinegar (see below) and poof, it's gone.

White vinegar and essential oil

Vinegar is a natural acid that quickly removes soap film, odors, baking soda grit, and is said to have germ-killing properties to boot! The only downside of vinegar is that it stinks. That's why we add the essential oils to make this a cleaning product you'll want to use all over your nest.

Make me: Use only white distilled vinegar—Heinz is best because it's made from corn and isn't a petroleum product like most others. Pour it into a clean spray bottle and add essential oil to your nose's taste.

Use me: Vinegar cuts through soapy residues on vinyl floors, sinks, tubs, showers, and shower curtains. These residues, usually a by-product of conventional cleaning products, attract dirt and make you have to clean more often, so get rid of them. Vinegar also neutralizes odors. Spray this sumptuous solution on carpets, sheets, or sofas. If you're using a baking soda cleanser (above) and are left with a gritty residue, spray this on and it'll dissolve away.

Baking soda, vinegar, soap & essential oil

Take the cleaning power of baking soda and vinegar, add a liquid soap, and you have a residue-dissolving, super-cleaning, soft-scrubbing product that works anywhere and everywhere.

Make me: Pour ½ cup of a high-quality liquid soap into a bowl (Dr. Bronner's liquid soap is a good choice). Then add about 1⅔ cups baking soda, and ½ cup water. Add 2 tablespoons white vinegar last, as vinegar ruins soap when added directly to it. Add the oil of your liking, then stir together, adding more water if necessary, until it's thin enough to pour into a clean, 16-oz. squirt bottle.

Use me: This solution is good for any dirty, greasy, grimy, soap-filmy job you've got! Use it in tubs and sinks; on countertops and stoves; even on vinyl, tile, and ceramic floors.

Scrub green: Dr. Bronner's Magic Soaps

Dr. Bronner's liquid soaps have achieved an almost cultlike status among eco-minded folks. Maybe it's the spiritual discourse he prints all over his labels, using quotes from Mohammed to Marx to push his utopian visions. Maybe it's the fact that his soap is so darn good—one drop goes a long way to gently clean everything from body parts to kitchen floors to laundry to teeth (yuck). Or maybe it's the fact that Dr. Bronner puts 10 percent of the company's profits toward charities. Whatever the reason, his soaps are available at natural food stores (or at www.drbronner.com) and come in fabulous scents like peppermint, lavender, tea tree, and eucalyptus.

Club soda

It's not just for cocktails anymore! Plain club soda is an ammonia-free hit when it comes to washing mirrors, windows, eyeglasses, chrome, and glass tables. The magic ingredient? Club soda contains sodium citrate, which softens water and helps it clean. Try it for yourself!

Make me: Get your pencils ready for this one: pour plain club soda into any clean spray bottle, or keep it in the store-bought bottle and just pour it on a clean rag when you need it.

Use me: Spray onto and wipe off of all the glass in the house. If you're cleaning chrome fixtures, put a few drops of vegetable oil on a rag, pour on club soda, and admire your spot-free reflection. Use along with Dr. Bronner's liquid soap to help wipe out fresh stains on clothes and carpets.

Olive oil, vinegar & lemon

Sound like a salad dressing? This simple recipe is actually a delicious dressing for your wood and leather furniture. While most furniture polishes use plastics to make your furniture look shiny, this actually restores the natural oils of wood and leather while whisking away that pesky dust. Don't use this recipe on your wood floors; it will leave a residue.

Make me: Take 2 teaspoons light olive oil, 1 teaspoon fresh lemon juice, and ¼ cup white distilled vinegar and pour them into a clean, 16-oz. spray bottle. Fill it to the top with water, and shake. Because of the lemon juice, this will need to be refrigerated; if you use essential lemon oil it doesn't.

Use me: Use to condition and clean any wood surfaces in the house (except your floors): furniture, cabinets, paneling, you name it. Also works on leather couches, shoes, and motorcycle jackets!

Clearing spaces

So, you've given your nest a good scrubbing, but it still feels dirty somehow. It may be polluted with the last tenant's energies, which calls for a good space-clearing ceremony. In many cultures, it's absolutely unthinkable to move into a home before it's been cleared of old energies, fortunes, misfortunes, and behavior patterns. It's also a good idea to cleanse your nest after you've been sick, depressed, or dumped; or if you've just been sitting on the sofa bingeing on too many *The Bachelor* reruns and Ben & Jerry's. Get it all out of your system!

Smudge it

Smudging has long been practiced by Native Americans to cleanse people and places of negative energies. The idea is that when an herbal smudge stick is burned, it releases smoke that attaches itself to negative energies and then clears them. To prepare a proper smudging, call around to natural-food and alternative-healing stores to find a good smudge stick. It will usually contain delicious dried herbs such as lavender, cedar, and sage, but it varies. Ask what the herbs in each smudge stick are for and pick the ones that are right for you. Then go back to your nest, light the stick, and smudge every room of its bad mojo.

Incense

Incense is similar to smudging, and has long been used by everyone from hipsters to hippies to the Pope as a way to purify space. Choose natural incense, not synthetic, which is heavily perfumed. Sandalwood, sage, cedar, frankincense, and myrrh are some of the best for space clearing. Light a stick or a cone or tablet, fan the smoke around you, breathe it in. Carry it through each of your rooms, purifying them of any stinky ol' stagnant energy.

Fire

Fire consumes, transcends, and purifies. Lighting candles is a powerful way to space-clear, sans the smokiness of smudging or incense. Place a lit votive candle on the floor of each room of your nest. Then light one main candle, hold it in your hands, and walk from room to room, focusing on clearing out negative energies. Allow each of the votives to slowly burn out.

Water

Water is the most powerful symbol of cleansing, and a little sprinkling of holy water is a great way to instantly cleanse negative energy. Even if you've already cleansed your nest, it's always nice to have a bowl of holy water lying around somewhere, as it evokes a calming, positive energy. Don't worry, you don't have to put on your Sunday dress to get your hands on some—you can make your own. (This holy water is infused with the powers of nature, and isn't necessarily religious.)

DIY "holy water": Spring water works, as does any store-bought water that's been bottled at the source, but only if the water is in a glass container, never plastic, never metal. You can also collect rainwater in glass or ceramic containers, but make sure it's been raining a while, early rainwater is dirty. Once you have your water, place it outside in the morning sunlight and infuse it with the sun's vibrant energy, or outside on a clear, moonlit night to charge it with the moon's healing energy; on a clear, moonless night it will absorb stellar dreams.

Got holy water? Now for the ceremony. Dip your fingers in your holy water and sprinkle yourself with it. Then focus on your cleansing efforts, and walk around each room of the house and sprinkle every nook and cranny. Be careful with hardwood floors; you may want to wipe up if you're a messy sprinkler.

Consider your nest cleansed.

Feather Your Nest

A few years ago, I was lucky enough to travel around Southeast Asia for six months. I boxed up all of my belongings, moved out of my house, and backpacked through Nepal, India, Thailand, Indonesia, and Malaysia. The whole time I was traveling, I collected precious objects that reminded me of people I had met, places I had seen, and misadventures I had survived. I picked up a clamshell as thick as my fist on a beach in Thailand, a gorgeous oil painting of the Buddha in Nepal, hand-carved wooden masks in Malaysia, prayer wheels and glass beads in India, and a piece of Mt. Bromo in Indonesia. I collected so many memories, I had to buy a second backpack to carry them all. I wore this "goodie bag" on the front of my body like a baby carrier until the weight and heat got the best of me. I ended up sending everything home via the slow boat to America, and upon my return, I had tons of precious goodies waiting for me. I'll never forget opening those boxes in my new home. The smells and memories of my trip came pouring out of those beat-up cardboard packages like perfume out of *Vogue*. And now, every time I look at the Malaysian masks on my wall, the Indian glass beads dangling in my bedroom doorway, and the Thai clamshell holding bath salts, I think of that trip, and what a wonderful time it was in my life.

Set the scene

When it comes to our personal lives, most of us lean toward one particular scene or feel or vibe. You either like nigiri sushi or chicken fried steak; fuzzy pastel sweaters or torn Day-Glo tights; Ravi Shankar or Lynrd Skynrd; vintage American Fords or Saabs. We like what we like, our scene grounds us and defines who we are. Understanding your scene can really help when it comes time to fill and feather your nest.

Your nest is where you lounge, love, laugh, and live your life. You're not sending any messages to anyone except yourself, so make sure your nest is all you. How to do this? Well, let's start with how not to do it. Don't rush out and buy the cheapest sofa, chair, and table set on display. You want to fill your nest with objects you buy out of love and not out of desperation. Your pickiness doesn't mean your furnishings have to be pricey; they just have to be the right fit.

But sometimes time is the enemy. Maybe you find yourself volunteering to throw your parents' anniversary dinner before realizing you have no dining room table—or chairs. Or maybe you just can't stand looking at your empty living room a day longer. When time is the issue, the key is to choose a scene and start with basic pieces (a sofa, chair, table, and lamp) that work well together. Say you start with Domestic Diva basics—a cream sofa, chambray-striped chair, and simple wooden table. Next week you can spice it up with a stack of red silk pillows for Global Girl flair, or a faux leopard-skin throw for a Rocker Grrl note, or a pink shag rug for a splash of Powerpuff Girl. It's all good. You can add and subtract artwork, rugs, drapes, and knickknacks to your little heart's desire—those original anchor pieces will always help tie it all together.

Here are a few fabulous nesting scenes to peruse, along with quick and simple furnishing ideas to help give your nest a quick burst of flavor. Pick one scene and run with it, or even better—mix and match as you please for a brilliant scene infusion!

Fusion

Remember how much fun it was to color outside the lines? The same goes for feathering your nest. Don't follow all the rules; mix it all up. Keep your decorating ideas fun, fresh, and eclectic. After all, you want it to represent you, right?

Global gal

You, your friends, and your things are electrically eclectic. You celebrate diversity and individuality, and your passion for unusual texture, color, and style knows no boundaries. Your nest is a display of the globally gorgeous: Mexican glassware, framed pictures of far-away lands, jewel-colored fabrics and pillows, carved incense holders, handcrafted Buddha statues, seashells collected from your beach trips. While your nine-to-five may not allow you to roam the world as much as you'd like, you pick up intriguing, otherworldly pieces wherever you go—even if it's just to Urban Outfitters.

The goods:

* Red and gold
* Prayer beads on door handles
* Batik fabric thrown over sofa
* Bright silk pillows (page 72)
* Piñatas
* Mojitos
* Buddha heads
* Faux bamboo furniture
* Saris as room dividers
* Japanese low table and Zen cushions
* Foreign newspapers on coffee table
* Kimono

Kitsch chick

You swoon for styles of the past, and you're drawn to things that are so bad, they're awesome. You and your pals gas up the Ranchero every weekend and brake for thrift stores and garage sales—the hunt is part of the thrill. Like a low-budget B-movie, you've accumulated a little bit of everything: the tiki cup that now holds your MAC brushes, ashtrays from old Super 8 motels, an original Farrah Fawcett *Charlie's Angels* doll—and you scored it all on the cheap. You could spend pocketfuls of cash on new retro-style stuff, but why do that when Value Village has 30 percent off red tags every Thursday?

The goods:

* Bright plastic and chrome
* Tiki anything
* Elvis is in the house
* Scooby-Doo lunchbox collection
* Vinyl (furniture and records)
* Fiesta dinnerware

* Chenille blanket over old sofa
* '50s furniture with spiky legs
* Gingham café curtains
* Retro magazine rack
* Rotary phone
* Vintage apron

Powerpuff girl

Pink is powerful, femme is fabulous. These days, a gal can have her pink fuzzy sweater with matching legwarmers and a BA from Harvard, too! Hooray for pink, hooray for romance, hooray for you, Powerpuff Girl. You enjoy sumptuous, soft fabrics like satin and feathers and velvets (oh my!) and you pamper yourself with girly goods straight out of a Marilyn Monroe movie: perfume, fuzzy slippers, lipstick, and pearls. Although you're feisty and plenty independent, you have a hankering for the old-fashioned boys who bring flowers, open doors, and buy you dirty martinis.

The goods:

* Pinks, pastels, florals
* Tickly feather boas over chairs
* Ballerina slippers hanging on the wall
* Vintage perfume bottles
* Harlequin Romances on heart-shaped coffee table
* Lipstick kisses on mirrors

* Heart pillows (page 72)
* A dozen red roses you sent yourself
* Fringe
* Princess canopy bed
* Framed pictures of you and your beau everywhere
* Pink satin hot pants

Rocker grrl

If you can barely put down those drumsticks long enough to read this, you know what scene you cling to. From Cyndi Lauper to Sleater-Kinney, Pat Benatar punk-head bands to pretty-in-pink tights—Rocker Grrls are taking the world (and the stage) by storm. Fiercely independent, driven, and fearless, you and your friends are always catching new bands or playing new gigs; you don't spend much time doing your nails or waiting for boys to call (unless the polish is metallic blue and the boy is Jack White). In both your nest and personal life, you embrace good music, good friends, and anything with attitude. As Madonna once screamed, "I wanna rule the world!" As do you, Rocker Grrl.

The goods:

* Red and black
* Black candles
* Zebra-print blanket over sofa
* Faux leopard rug & pillows (page 74)
* Guitar straps as curtain holders
* Joan Jett coasters
* Bandanas tied around chairs
* Sheet music wallpaper (page 21)
* Classic rock posters
* Red flames appliquéd on chairs
* Guitar-pick picture frames
* Black leather pants

Dot-com darlin'

Hi-tech meets modern minimalist—that's you, Dot-Com Darlin'. You spend oh-too-much time at your day job staring at a monitor, so when you come home, you want things uncluttered, straightforward, and simple. Your personal life, like your professional persona, is well organized, scheduled, and without a lot of loose strings, but this doesn't keep you from letting go with your friends every weekend. You're techy but love the finer things in life like Italian coffee, directors' cuts, and remastered CDs. You're glued to a Titanium Power-Book from eight to five, but once that whistle blows, watch out, boys! Dot-Com Darlin' in the house!

The goods:

* Stainless and brick
* Framed manga collection
* Computer desk made from old door
* Steel coffee table with stack of remotes
* Black pleather sofa
* CD jewel-box picture holders
* Beanbags
* Cappuccino parties
* Geometric designs painted on wall (page 21)
* Geometric mobile
* Organizers for your organizers
* Zipper-stretch cargos

Domestic diva

You've got the bob, the Hold Everything and Pottery Barn cards, the Jetta wagon, and an affinity for neutrals—you're a Domestic Diva. You can't get enough of fresh-cut flowers from your own garden, home crafts, dinner parties, decorating tips—you can spend hours in your nest arranging and cooking and purring the day away, except for the occasional road trip to Home Depot, that is.

The goods:

* The colors sage and cream
* Postcards from the Hamptons on fridge
* Chambray slipcover on sofa
* Little bowls full of potpourri
* Pictures in hanging ribbon frames
* Killer cookware set
* Coverlets and bedskirts
* Vintage rolling pin collection
* Herb garden (page 94)
* Framed pressed flowers
* Padded coat hangers
* Khakis

Ten things every nest needs

A nest just isn't a nest without the basics. Some are pretty obvious, such as furniture, lighting, and knickknacks, but please don't forget the less-than-lovely necessities such as a good toolbox and stocked emergency kit. Remember, you want your nest to be fashionable, but functional.

1. Furniture. A sofa, chair, and table are perhaps the first pieces you want to pick up for your nest. This way, you can start having friends over pronto and they won't have to sit on the floor (bad hostess!). Plus, you can always crash on your sofa if you have yet to land a bed. A sofa is the centerpiece of any living space so pick one carefully. If buying secondhand, you can always throw a sheet, funky fabric, or slipcover over it, but make sure it's comfy and that the cushions don't already have butt-prints as deep as the Grand Canyon.

   Tip: As far as furniture goes, use your imagination. A stack of art books makes a lovely coffee table; chop off a table's legs for an instant Japanese low table; take red, white, and blue duct tape to a vinyl couch and make a rockin' American (or Brit) flag sofa!

   Tip: It doesn't have to have legs to be a seat. Think silk beanbags, Zen-like floor cushions, yoga balls, prayer rugs, and ottomans slipcovered in velvet.

   Tip: If you find a sofa that's perfect save for a few stains and light smells, you can rent a rug cleaner at a supermarket or home center. Many of them come with upholstery attachments.

2. Light. Do you want a lamp for light's sake or for look's sake? There are as many different lamp styles and light sources as there are bad Bruce Willis movies: modern floor lamps, Asian-inspired paper lamps that hang from the ceiling, torchieres, wall sconces, retro tiki lamps, studious desk lamps, Christmas lights, candles, even lava lamps!

   You never want to flood an entire room in bright light—

think ambience, baby, ambience. Mix and match your fixture and bulb choices so that you layer two different types of light: ambient and task. Ambient light fills an entire room, but may be too dim to knit by. Task lighting (usually from smaller fixtures with brighter bulbs) fills dark corners, highlights objects d'art, and illuminates task areas such as card tables and reading chairs.

Tip: Mirrors are a girl's best friend when it comes to lighting. A big mirror with candles, a lava lamp, or a string of chili pepper lights in front of it will spread the warm, soft light around beautifully.

A good bulb

Yellow lightbulbs cast a flattering warm glow during dinner parties, but it's the white bulb that helps you clean up the chip crumbs in the carpet come morning. Mix your bulbs: yellow bulbs in dining and living areas, white bulbs in home offices and kitchens, and how about a red bulb in the boudoir? Forget about fluorescent bulbs; the light is so unflattering.

---

3. Window dressing. Floor-length curtains look fabulously elegant; buy them long and let the fabric puddle on the floor for a romantic flair. Short café curtains cover the bottom halves of the windows and give you privacy while still letting in light. But why not throw tradition out the window? Layer pieces of silk, chintz, lace, or sheer fabric for deliciously sheer texture; or make curtains out of vintage scarves, pink bandanas, or rock Ts. Sew seashells, beads, or other funky items onto fabric, or string dried flowers or glass butterflies onto fishing line and hang in front of (or instead of) fabric for kitschy texture. Don't forget the romance of the valance—you can have plenty of fun twisting and braiding and stapling fabric up above the window, too.

Tip: Draped fabric can also make for an elegantly effective room divider. Screw in a curtain rod anywhere and use floor-length fabric to hide messy shelves, television and computer areas, to divide a living area from a kitchen area, or to create an instant meditation space.

Tip: Curtains not your style? Stack glass blocks against the window; buy a DIY stained-glass kit; find an old stained-glass window and lean it against your existing window; or buy window paints (like supermarkets use for holidays) and make window art. Shades and blinds are nice to look at but can run on the pricey side.

4. Magic carpets. An exotic wool carpet from Morocco can literally whisk you away to another place and time—but the trip isn't cheap. Prayer rugs and yoga mats make nice, inexpensive floor coverings that friends can sit on, and they store easily. For a funky, functional rug on the cheap, try thrift stores. You can always have a rug cleaned, or sew on new trim or fringe to spice it up. If a new shag is more your style, Urban Outfitters, Target, and IKEA offer a bevy of different colors, shapes, sizes, and textures. An alternative to rugs is natural matting. Popular in Asia, matting is eco-friendly, blends into any decorating scheme, provides good insulation, and feels great under the feet! Sea grass, husks, and jute are just some of the plants used for matting, and Pier 1 Imports or any import store is a good place to look.

Tip: If you have concrete floors, paint them! It's not as warm as a rug, but nothing spices up a room like a hand-painted mandala on the floor.

5. Wall candy. Hands down, the best place to look for art is at G-sales (slang for garage sales), stoop sales (a New York–style G-sale), or any thrift store. There are motherloads of cheap and undiscovered artistic treasure in secondhand stores: velvet Elvis paintings, folk art, oil portraits, B&W photographs of people you don't know, cute kitsch handkerchiefs begging to be framed—it's endless! Have a frame you fancy but can't find the right piece of art to put in it? Just hang the empty frame, and then drape a piece of fabric or scarf over it and let it spill down the sides. But also think outside the frame when it comes to art.

Perk up any wall by hanging vintage plates, Asian fans, dried floral bouquets, hats, record albums, strings of beads, mirrors, vintage fabrics, and scarves. Add some texture by covering a wall in faux fur, the racier the better. Paint a wall with magnetic paint and spell out words du jour with alphabet magnets, or paint a pink unicorn and bring back the '70s.

Tip: Sometimes it's not what's in the frames but the frames themselves. Glue guitar picks, buttons, dice, or glitter to any frame for instant wall candy.

6. Bric-a-brac. Driftwood and seashells, vintage snowglobes, Beanie Babies, little glass poodles, hand-carved wooden masks from Indonesia—whatever knickknacks you collect, always display them with pride. In order to keep them from looking cluttered, arrange by topic, color, texture, or shape. Like holiday decorations, knickknacks can work best on a rotating schedule. Bring the aloha display down from the attic in the spring, and cozy up for the winter with stay-indoor items like Easy Bake Ovens and vintage board game collections!

7. Plants. Whether it's a bottle garden, an herb garden, a bonsai tree, or a window box—plants rock. Not only do they clean the air we breathe, they bring life and warmth into every nest. So you're not exactly Jane of the Jungle and every plant you've

If you can't duct it, f#@! it

Originally invented to keep moisture out of ammunition cases during World War II, duct tape has gone on to become the one-and-only cult tape. It's been used to make prom dresses, furniture, leg-waxing strips, and temporary roofs, and to fix just about anything from engines to broken stilettos to thatch huts in South America. Duck brand duct tape is my personal favorite. It sticks the best, and comes in cool colors like blaze orange, hot pink, lime green, and camouflage. Duct tape the top of your coffee table hot pink and black, camo-tape your thigh-highs, or just repair your leaky pipes—but whatever you do, check out what Jim and Tim have to say at www.DuctTapeGuys.com. Believe me, you'll learn something!

ever owned died? Try, try again! Plants that tolerate low levels of sunlight are the easiest to care for. Most houseplants like some sun, but not the direct sun from sitting on a windowsill—the window acts like a magnifying glass. First thing to do when you take a plant home from the nursery? Ditch that drab plastic planter! Dig around thrift stores for cool teapots, cups and saucers, cookie jars, and sugar bowls to proudly front your foliage (more about plants on page 95).

Tip: Put plants in front of rusty radiators, holes in the wall, or over spots in the carpet for instant camouflage.

Tip: Wood and water don't mix. Whenever putting a potted plant on a hardwood floor, always put something between the two, like a slab of cork.

8. Tool kit. Attention nesters: true independence requires self-sufficiency, which means it's time you learn to fix leaky faucets and blown fuses on your own, without speed-dialing your daddy. Get a good fix-it book like *The Woman's Hands-On Home Repair Guide* by Lyn Herrick, and assemble yourself a basic toolbox pronto. Here are a few basic tools every box needs: hammer, straight-slot screwdriver, Phillips-head screwdriver, pliers, adjustable wrench or socket wrench, utility knife, steel tape measure, duct tape, box of nails, box of screws, and a can of WD-40. Sears is still my favorite place to buy tools; ask a salesperson to help you assemble the perfect first-timer's kit if necessary. Just don't skimp on quality—the right toolbox can be passed down to your granddaughters!

9. Emergency kit. Remember Y2K? Hordes of frenzied, freaked-out individuals raced to their nearest store to stock up on canned goods, drinking water, candles, batteries, and tampons. Shelves were empty, and long story short, fear spreads faster than wildfire. May I suggest you stock up on emergency supplies before The Big One, while the vibe is calm and the shelves are fully stocked. Go to www.redcross.org for a list of emergency items you should have stashed at all times. And don't stop there. I've got an emergency stash of red wine, playing cards, and chocolate bars in my disaster relief kit. How about you?

10. Love. Last but definitely not least—you've painted and cleaned and cleansed and filled, and now you're sitting around looking at your lovely new lair wondering, what next? I'll tell you what's next—share the love! It's time to start entertaining, creating memories, and scuffing up those newly cleaned hardwood floors. Throw a nest-warming bash that makes your friends a permanent part of your nest. Have a finger-painting party and let friends decorate one lonely wall, or provide the supplies (and wine) and let them make handmade artwork for your walls. The morning after your soiree, you'll be surrounded by new memories, and even more conversation pieces!

Secondhand chic

No matter what I'm hunting for, be it furniture, dishes, artwork, or fabric for pillows—I always start my goodie hunt with a sweep of my fave thrift stores. Plaid sofas can be slipcovered in velvet, torn love seats can be appliquéd, dressers can be painted, artwork can be re-framed, almost anything can be cleaned—thrift stores are a regular gold mine for the crafty, style-conscious gal. Found objects have so much more personality than vacuum-packed, fresh-from-the-factory items, and they also leave you with latte money to spare. Pick up those Yellow Pages, look under Thrift or Secondhand Stores, get the girls together, and make a day of it!

An often overlooked source of secondhand chic is your local antique expo. Contrary to popular belief, these events are not just for serious collectors looking to drop a thou. They almost always offer a bevy of wonderfully odd and useful objects at great prices. I've seen old fences, mannequins, tools, weathered furniture with great bone structure, iron skillets, linens, vintage coat hooks, you name it. Antique expos tour the country much like a circus; check your local paper to see when one's coming to town. And don't forget to browse the goods at your local garage sales and stoop sales. One gal's trash, another gal's pleasure.

So feng shui

Romance problems? Shrinking savings account? Depressed? Nothing that a little feng shui can't cure. Feng shui is the Taoist art and science of living in harmony with your environment. It works on the principle that the energy of your nest—its colors, furniture arrangement, layout, shapes, materials, and even location—all have a constant influence on your energy state. Feng shui helps improve your life by balancing your chi, or life-force energy, with the chi of your environment. There are many schools of thought concerning feng shui, but basic principles include balancing the five elements: earth, metal, water, wood, and fire; and the Ba-Gua, a universal diagram that assigns each area of the house a specific purpose: career, knowledge, family, wealth, fame, marriage, children, and health. Ever wonder why so many Chinese restaurants have aquariums in the entryways? An aquarium (water) stimulates wealth chi when placed in the career Gua (the entryway) of a building. It's a bit mathematical, but feng shui has some fabulous insights and quick fixes for just about any ailment in your life. Having a hard time getting a grip on life? Check and fix any loose door handles. Lonely? Hang a wind chime over your bed and sauce up your love life. Broke? Fix a leak in your finances by fixing any leaky faucets. Living in too-cramped of a space? Hang a crystal prism from the ceiling. Feeling tired? Perk up your health Gua (the central area) with plants, or paint the area yellow, orange, or brown. These tips are just the beginning; get a book to find out more ways to re-groove your nest so that it works for you—*Practical Feng Shui* by Simon Brown is an easy-to-understand read. In the meantime, don't put a TV or waterbed in your boudoir. They are so not feng shui.

PART TWO

··

Fly Solo

Believe it or not, the first time I ever lived alone was when I moved to New York City. In a mega-metropolis where almost two million people literally live on top of each other and pay exorbitant rents for shoe-box apartment shares, I just plain lucked out and landed myself an (almost) affordable, two-bedroom apartment, walking distance from New York's finest theaters, restaurants, and the bustle of Times Square. Of course, this two-bedroom New York apartment was smaller than a studio on the West Coast, a touch on the grungy side, and my kitchen was the size of a closet, but I wasn't complaining. I had the whole place to myself, with the exception of the two lap cats that came with the place. I could dance to '80s music in the middle of the night, ignore the dishes in the sink, and watch *The Simple Life* without anybody ever knowing. But I had trouble adapting to my newly proclaimed "solo lifestyle." All of New York was literally right at my feet, but after having roommates my whole life, my new bachelorette pad felt quiet and empty. I had friends in New York, but I was on a budget and couldn't go out every night of the week. I knew I had to find a way to occupy myself in my new "nest for

one"—to save money, to save cell phone minutes, and to save me from becoming addicted to *Sex and the City* reruns.

* * *

Let's get crafty!

You've slept in on a wonderfully lazy Sunday afternoon, sucked down your second latte, and taken an honorable stab at the local paper's crossword puzzle—now what's a girl to do? Get crafty with it! Home spas, knitting, sewing, scrapbooking, growing herb gardens, flower arranging—these domestic DIY activities aren't just for Carol Brady anymore. You'll be surprised at what a little imagination, inspiration, and patience will do for your nest, and your state of mind to boot!

A smidgen of glue and paper can turn your shoeboxes full of old high school photos into a fun, funky scrapbook. A little soil, water, and love can sprout an herb garden that will season your dinner parties with fresh, homemade flavor every time. If you can thread a needle, you can transform your drab, dusty pillows into exotic beauties straight out of Arabian Nights. Think you can't sew a stitch or organize a crafty activity to save your life? You've just found, filled, and feathered an entire nest, for goodness' sake. Keep that motor running! Get your scissors, glue, and imagination out of the box and rev up for a bevy of fun and fabulous ideas anyone can whip up in a jiffy.

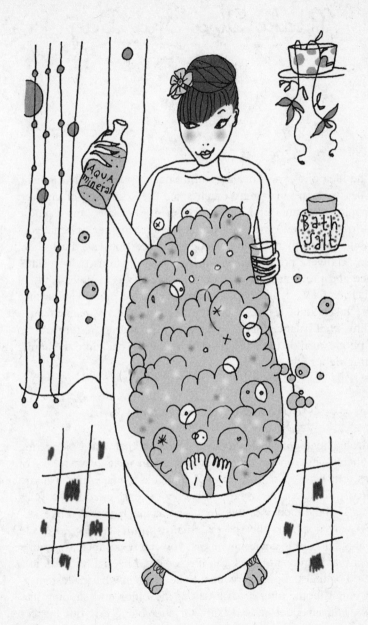

Make It a Spa Day

The idea of a spa, a healing, nurturing, pampering environment, has been around pretty much since the beginning of civilized humanity. The ancient Egyptians, Romans, Persians, and Chinese (just to name a few) were all keen to the amazing health benefits of massage, aromatherapy, and a long soak in a hot bath. Back then, these acts were not considered a luxury so much as daily maintenance and preventative medicine. It's only in recent times, and especially in the West, that the spa experience has become an indulgence to be taken outside the home, rather than part of maintaining a healthy, well-balanced life. I say we take an afternoon, turn off the cell phone, turn on the music, and bring the spa back into the home, starting right now.

Your very own home spa

Aromatherapeutic oils, scented baths, herbal teas, pampering treatments—just one afternoon at a spa can melt away weeks of stress and leave you in a state of pure bliss. But while spas are wickedly fabulous, they're also wickedly expensive, and most folks can't afford the money or the time to go as much as they'd like.

So why not bring the spa experience home? It's easy to create a healing, nurturing environment that you can seek sanctuary in anytime, no appointment necessary. (Personally, I need a hot soak in a scented bath just about every night to keep me in whack.) Just imagine coming home after a toxic day at the office and slipping into a candlelit, lavender-infused bath. Or after being on your feet for hours, sipping on some hot herbal tea and treating yourself to a warm, rosemary footbath. Or having a whole afternoon to yourself, turning off your cell and treating yourself from your head (a honey-yogurt face pack) all the way down to your toes (a warm almond-oil dip). Of course, nothing can replace the indulgent feeling of spending an afternoon rubbing elbows with the beautiful people at a professional spa, but read on for ideas that will definitely keep you tided over in between visits—or at least for an afternoon. Some of the following ideas are as instant and easy as adding a few drops of essential oil into a hot bath, and some take a bit more preparation and patience, like making your own essential oils. But they're all wonderfully relaxing and indulgent, and you're worth it.

First step: clean

The first step to making any bathroom into a spa is to (gulp) clean it. Think of it as revamping your bathroom to serve your spiritual needs. Scrub your floor, sink, shelves, and tub; and be sure to use the aromatherapeutic cleaning-product recipes from page 29. They'll make your bathroom start looking and smelling like a spa right off the bat.

Appease the senses

The key to your home spa's success is to think big picture with your pampering plan. Visualize your spa in terms of an overall experience, not just the act of lighting a few candles or taking a simple bath. For a truly blissful experience, you want to lightly appease all five senses: sight, smell, hearing, touch, and taste. The following home-spa how-to's are broken down as to how they tickle all five fabulous senses. You need not do all of them; they are only there to guide you into a well-balanced, euphoric afternoon or evening.

1. Make it look good

Clutter: Stand in the doorway and look at your bathroom—really look at it. Are there rows of plastic, packaged products on display?

Are there stacks of magazines on the back of the toilet? Toothpaste spray all over the mirror? An uncluttered bathroom makes for an uncluttered mind. Take any bright packages and needless plastic bottles and store them under the counter. Put all of your toiletries in the medicine cabinet. Put cotton balls, Q-tips, and bath salts on display in glass containers. Remove all dirty clothing, towels, and washcloths. Only display your thickest towels, and instead of just folding them and stacking them, roll them up like a yoga mat first—very Zen!

Lighting: If you have fluorescent lights in your bathroom, turn them off when it comes to spa time. Both the light and the buzzing sound of fluorescent bulbs are terrible and have no place in your new spa. If you have soft light, that's okay; but hands down, nothing beats candles in the bathroom. Candlelight is ambient, relaxing, and meditative. Set up a line of votive candles on your shelves or along the edge of your tub, or get a stand-up candle holder so you can read in the bath. Stay away from heavily perfumed candles though. You'll be using essential oils in your new spa, and heavy or synthetic candle fragrances might not mix that well.

2. Make it smell good

Incense & burners: Incense can help you slip in or out of any mood. Just avoid heavy-scented synthetic incense, and remember to burn it outside your bathroom so you don't smoke yourself out. To avoid the smoke issue altogether, try oil burners. They're another great way to fragrance a room. Just fill the metal bowl with water, add a few drops of your oil du jour, and light the candle underneath. You can also put a bowl of scented water on a heated radiator, or a few drops on a lightbulb for a similar effect.

Essential oils: Essential oils are the captured, vital-life essence of aromatic plants, and they have a powerful place in your spa. Be aware that each oil has its own effects, and you want to make the oils work for your state of mind at the time. You wouldn't want to put peppermint oil into your bedtime bath as it might keep you up all night—calming clary-sage oil would be a much better choice. Always try to get the highest-grade oils (therapeutic grade is the best, see page 28), buy them in small quantities, and store them in a cool,

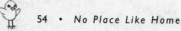

dark place. Also, test for any skin reaction before you dip your entire body in a bath full of the stuff!

The power of oils: Aromatherapy harnesses the powers of essential oils to improve the mind, body, and spirit. Here are some of the more common oils and their powers that be.

Bergamot: Squeezed out of the peel of a bitter green orange, bergamot refreshes and lifts the spirit. It's good for acne, oily skin and hair, and dandruff, but it does make skin sun-sensitive.

Chamomile: This oil is renowned for calming rashes, the mind, and dry skin. It can also be used with hot water as a compress for cramps.

Clary sage: The fresh, herby aroma induces a calming, drowsy state, and is great for a nighttime bath. It's also good for aches and pains, respiratory problems, and oily skin.

Eucalyptus: If you have a cold, a few drops of this sweet, menthol oil in a hot bath will help clear congestion. Add a few drops to some body oil and rub it on your chest after the bath for a good night's sleep.

Frankincense: From the boswellia tree in Arabia, this sweet, woodsy oil is rejuvenating and relaxing at the same time; it's also beneficial to chapped and aging skin.

Geranium: A spicy floral oil that helps with menstrual and menopausal problems, boosts circulation (good for the skin), and can be used as an aphrodisiac (draw your bath for two!).

Ginger: Spicy and pungent, ginger is a good warm-me-up when added to a hot bath and relieves muscle aches and cramps. Also good for chills, colds, and flu.

Grapefruit: Whenever your spirits need a little lift, grab the grapefruit. This fresh, zingy oil increases circulation and helps with depression, headaches, and stress.

Jasmine: An uplifting oil that encourages optimism and self-confidence. It's also good for muscle pains, cramps, anxiety, and depression.

Lavender: A calming oil that makes all your worries go down the drain with the bathwater. It soothes swollen feet and sprains, is good for dry skin, and makes a great after-sunburn bath.

Lemon: Lemon oil boosts circulation as it sharpens the mind and helps you make choices. It's also good for brightening blonde hair, but stay out of the sun after using it.

Neroli: This oil is obtained from the flowers of the orange tree, and its spicy, sweet-bitter scent is sensual and relaxing. Also helps smooth wrinkles and stretch marks.

Orange: The sweet, perky aroma puts you in a better mind-set by banishing negative thoughts and easing stress.

Patchouli: This spicy, musky oil is known for its sensual, arousing qualities. Use just a little as an aphrodisiac; too much will act as a sedative or a Grateful Dead show flashback.

Peppermint: This cool, minty oil awakens the senses and lifts the spirits. Try a peppermint bath in the morning instead of a cup of coffee!

Rose: Rose oil provides a sense of calm and well-being and is used as a treatment for menstrual and menopausal problems.

Rosemary: This woodsy oil stimulates the brain and helps fight drowsiness; great for a morning bath or before a long night out. Also promotes hair growth and fights dandruff.

Sandalwood: This sweet, musky oil eases depression, stress, and insomnia. It also inspires creativity, is an aphrodisiac, and is known to be kind to dry, chapped skin.

Ylang-ylang: This spicy-sweet oil is a renowned aphrodisiac; it's also used to overcome fear, frustration, anxiety, and depression.

DIY oils: These homemade oils won't be as strong as the ones you purchase, but they're still nice, and custom-made by you! Always start with fresh flower petals, lemon peel, ginger-root shavings, lavender flowers, or whatever you want to "juice"—dried samples just won't release enough essence. Take about 3 to 4 cups (you'll have to experiment with this) of your herb or flower, and smash it a bit with a mortar and pestle or rolling pin. This opens up the fibers and starts releasing the juices. Put the smashed pieces in an airtight glass container (dark glass is best). Pour in about ½ cup jojoba or apricot kernel oil, close it tightly, shake vigorously, and put the jar in a dark, cool place. Let it steep for thirty days, shaking at least once a week, then strain out fibers and check for skin sensitivity before you unleash its powers.

Oil cheat sheet

Normal skin:	Lavender, bergamot, rose, and jasmine
Oily skin:	Rosemary, eucalyptus, and frankincense
Sensitive skin:	Lavender, chamomile, and rose
Dry skin:	Sandalwood and rose
Breakouts:	Tea tree, lemon, and bergamot

Warning

Essential oils are powerful stuff. If you have a medical condition, are taking homeopathic remedies, or are pregnant or breast-feeding, please check with an aromatherapist before you use any oils. Also, always do a patch test on your skin before using.

---

3. Make it sound good

Forgetting the music on spa day is like forgetting the wine at a dinner party. Major buzzkill. Music has the power to help seduce you into the altered state of being you're so diligently seeking. Ambient music is always nice, as its meditative sounds carry the mood and blend into the background. Environmental CDs with sounds of raindrops, whales, the ocean, and thunderstorms can be quite soothing. World music is a good escape, particularly if you can't understand the words and just surrender to the music. Some days you might want the soft sounds of Norah Jones, others the exotic sounds of Anoushka Shankar's sitar. Sometimes you might want to groove to Groove Armada (particularly if you're going out later that night)— but do stay away from that radio dial. The commercials will only invade your happy place.

4. Make it feel good

Let's get physical. Let's slather our bodies in honey and yogurt, dip our feet in lavender and rosemary, scrub our skin with oatmeal and almonds, and then sit in a hot bath and let it all melt away. Remember, you can substitute the essential oils in these recipes as you wish, but please read the The Power of Oils section (page 55), and always test your skin for irritation before you put something all over your face.

Nourish: With a trip to a natural grocery store and a couple of hours, you can whip yourself up enough personalized home-spa treatments to fill an entire day in your planner! Read on for all-natural recipes that are good for your skin, good for your state of mind, and almost good enough to eat.

Mint & honey soy body pack

The honey moisturizes, and the peppermint helps clear the skin and boosts your energy level to boot. Good for dry skin.

Get it:

1 cup soy powder	1 tablespoon honey
1 cup plain yogurt	2–5 drops peppermint oil

Make it & use it: Mix together the soy powder, plain yogurt, and honey, then add the peppermint oil. Slather all over your body, wait twenty minutes (it won't dry), then dip yourself into a hot tub scented with the oil of your choice (rose is a nice complement). Use when fresh.

Chamomile French clay mask

The chamomile calms, the sweet almond oil moisturizes, and the French clay draws out impurities.

Get it:

1/8 cup French clay (available at natural food stores)	Water
	1–2 drops chamomile
1 teaspoon sweet almond oil	

Make it & use it: Mix the clay and almond oil, then add water until it makes a paste. Add the chamomile oil, and apply when fresh. Leave on face for twenty minutes, then rinse off. Good for all skin types.

Skin scrub

This salty concoction exfoliates, polishes, moisturizes—and leaves your skin smelling fabulous. Similar scrubs sell for $10 and up in stores, but you can make your own for a fraction of the price. Keeps in the shower for up to eight weeks.

Get it:

2 cups sea salt	4 teaspoons essential oil(s)
1/3 cup sweet almond oil	of choice
1/3 cup jojoba oil	

Make it: Combine the sea salt and oils in a large bowl. Add essential oils and blend. Put in an airtight container; clear is best because this looks so lovely.

Lavender shower scrub

The almond and oatmeal gently scrub away dead skin cells, the liquid soap cleanses, and the lavender calms. Use once or twice a week for glowing skin!

Get it:

- ¼ cup aloe vera gel
- ½ teaspoon liquid soap (liquid castile soap or Dr. Bronner's lavender soap; see page 30)
- 2 teaspoons ground almonds
- 2 teaspoons ground oatmeal flakes
- 1–2 drops lavender oil
- ½ teaspoon lavender flowers (optional)

Make it & use it: Just mix it all together and scrub 'til you shine. Put it in an airtight container (an old jelly jar works nicely), and it'll last in your shower about two weeks.

Sandalwood sweet almond oil hand & nail bath

The sandalwood rejuvenates and heals, the lavender calms, and the cypress smoothes your skin and nails. Oh, did I mention the almond oil moisturizes?

Get it:

- 5 tablespoons sweet almond oil
- 2 drops lavender oil
- 2 drops sandalwood oil
- 2 drops cypress oil

Make it & use it: Carefully warm the almond oil on the stove or in the microwave, and pour into a small bowl. Add the other oils; soak your hands for ten minutes. Give yourself a hand massage, then apply to feet, too! Use when fresh.

Warm rosemary footbath

This footbath is wonderful on tired, aching feet. It eases swelling and promotes general euphoria—add a little peppermint and it just may cure a headache!

Get it:

1 quart of water	3 drops rosemary oil
5 drops juniper oil	3 drops lavender oil

Make it & use it: Warm the water, add the oils, pour into a bowl big enough for both feet, and finally sit down and relax. Soak your feet for at least twenty minutes, then prop them up on pillows, and have your man fetch you some ice cream.

Ylang-ylang herbal dusting powder

This powder cools, smoothes, and makes your skin smell like an exotic treat. Keeps for up to two months.

Get it:

½ cup arrowroot powder	2 drops sandalwood oil
½ cup rice flour	1 drop neroli oil
1 drop ylang-ylang oil	

Make it & use it: Sift the powder and flour together, then add oil one drop at a time, sifting the whole mixture again after each drop. Put in a shaker container (an empty baby powder container works great), and store in a cool place. Dust it on after your bath, or sprinkle some on your sheets before you get into bed. Delish.

Lush-ous

If you'd rather buy your spa products instead of making them, go online and get yourself some Lush products. Their fresh, handmade

---

soaps, bubble bars, bath bombs, skin care products, and massage bars are all-natural, never tested on animals, and almost good enough to eat. When I slather Sympathy for the Skin banana-vanilla lotion on my legs, my dog follows me around and licks my heels. I've even known a few friends who couldn't resist licking a bar or two of Lush soap! Many Lush products are organic and even vegan. Previously available everywhere except the United States (Lush even has stores in Sri Lanka, South Korea, and Croatia!), Lush is finally opening stores in North America. Until one comes to your 'hood, you can order online at www.lush.com. Make sure to request a copy of the fabulously written and illustrated Lush Life catalog!

Soak: A leisurely, hot scented bath is the perfect complement to any home-spa treatment—or it can be a euphoric spa experience on its own. All you need is a tub, twenty minutes, and a few drops of essential oil, and you can have yourself a take-me-away moment any time of day. For a bath that's good for the skin as well as the soul, try one of the following recipes. Drop in the oils after the bath is full, otherwise the running water releases most of the fragrances before you even step in.

Normal skin: 4 drops neroli, 3 drops rose, 1 cup whole milk, 2 tablespoons honey

Oily skin: 5 drops basil, 2 drops lemon, 1 drop peppermint

Dry skin: 2 drops bergamot, 3 drops lavender, ½ cup apricot kernel oil, 1 teaspoon jojoba oil, and 2 tablespoons olive oil. **Note:** This recipe makes ½ cup, but you only need 1 tablespoon per bath

Party-girl detox bath: 2 drops geranium, 2 drops rosemary, 2 drops juniper

After-sun bath: 4 drops peppermint, 5 drops lavender, 2 tablespoons jojoba oil

Tip: Don't have a bathtub? You can still indulge in an aromatherapeutic experience. Get in the shower and use the Lavender Shower

Scrub recipe on page 60 (substitute any oils you wish). Once you get out of the shower, add a few drops of the same oils to an unscented body lotion and slather it on your skin. Touch up throughout the day with some Spa in a Bottle (page 66); you'll smell and feel fabulous!

5. Make it taste good

This is when the benefits of your home spa become deliciously obvious. Some foods are just as linked to your emotions and health as that neroli oil you just bathed in. Here are some ideas to pamper the last but not least of your senses, taste.

Herbal infusions

An infusion is a drink made from steeping leaves and flowers. Just pour boiling water over the bunch, cover, and steep for ten to thirty minutes, depending on how strong you like it. That's it. The liquid retains all of the plant's healing properties, and you've got yourself a nice little cup of bliss. Here are a few of my favorite infusions and their health benefits. Drink a cup or two after your bath to replenish liquids and vitality!

Anise: The seeds are sweet and licorice-like and help a tummy ache.

Chamomile: The flowers have a light, sweet taste and promote deep relaxation and sleep.

Cinnamon: The bark is warm and spicy and helps ease nausea and symptoms of colds and flu.

Dandelion: The leaves are bitter but are a good diuretic and blood cleanser.

Ginger: The root is spicy and good for relieving cramps and symptoms of colds and flu; also increases circulation.

 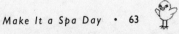

Lavender: The flowers soothe and calm the nerves and relieve fatigue and headaches.

Mint: The leaves refresh and cool on a hot day and help relieve cramps.

Nettle: The leaves purify and nourish the blood, improve energy, and decrease stress.

Rose: The leaves and flowers are relaxing and lift your spirits.

Sage: The leaves keep your brain sharp and memory quick, hence the name.

Chocolate

How many spas do you know of that serve chocolate as part of their mind/body treatment? Not many, but they should. Chocolate is known for its happiness-inducing properties, so be sure to include it in your spa day. After you've soaked, polished, and pampered, slip a little piece of chocolate on your tongue and surrender yourself to its sweet, savory goodness. Personally, I prefer rich, dark chocolate—it melts my worries into a little puddle on the floor.

Oh, honey!

Honey is hygroscopic, meaning it attracts water—that's why it's used in so many moisturizing skin products. Why not treat your tastebuds to this sticky-sweet treat as well? Honey is a quick energizer, and it's good for sore throats and coughs. Try drizzling a little clover honey on plain yogurt with roasted almonds; or vanilla ice cream with a dusting of cinnamon; or fresh fruit with chopped mint leaves. It's naturally delicious!

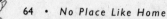

Sweet dreams

What a day. You've melted away your stress in a steamy, scented bath, soaked your fingers and toes in warm almond oil, listened to your favorite music, and sipped herbal tea. What better way to wrap up your session of bliss and pampering than to slip in between your sheets and rest your head near a soothing, lavender-and-rose-scented pillow? You'll wake up tomorrow refreshed, rejuvenated, and revived. That's a promise.

Herbal dream pillow

Get it:

1 cup dried chamomile   1 cup dried rose petals
1 cup dried lavender flowers   5 drops lavender oil

Make it & use it: Stir all ingredients together, put into a soft fabric sack, and sew opening shut. Put near your pillow, get some z's. Sweet dreams.

Spa express: If you're just too rushed or frazzled to think about throwing together a home spa experience, here's a surefire, thirty-minute plan for girls on the go:

Turn off your cell, put on your favorite CD, light some candles and some incense, or an oil burner if you have it. Apply a face mask or body treatment, sit down for five minutes, close your eyes, and just breathe. Focus on your breath as it flows in and out—clear your mind. Then run yourself a hot bath, and as the tub's filling, make yourself a nice cup of green or herbal tea. The mask should be dry now and the tub almost full—the perfect time to add oils of your choice and sink in. Soak for twenty minutes, and finish off with a dusting of herbal powder, spritzing of spray (see below), or your lotion or perfume of choice. You're refreshed and good to go!

Spa in a bottle

So, the boss has said you have to work all weekend, ruining your home-spa plans? Just take a piece of the spa with you! Blend 4 ounces of witch hazel with 1 teaspoon of your essential oil of choice, and pour into a travel-size spray bottle. Spray on your skin for a quick pick-you-up, anytime, anywhere.

Stitch with It

As far back as your mom, your grandma, and your grandma's grandma can probably remember, sewing and knitting have been deemed "women's work." I have no idea what's so belittling about the work that women do, but the point here is that before boutiques and Banana Republic, making clothes for the family was first and foremost the women's responsibility. If Pa needed a new pair of trousers and the baby-on-the-way a warm blanket, the wife and daughters got busy making them. Then something happened that would change this pattern forever: the Industrial Revolution made ready-to-wear clothing readily available, freeing Ma from her needles and allowing her to think about other things, like getting an education and having the girls over for bridge and cocktails. When the women's movement of the 1960s and '70s came about, droves of women left their nests for the corporate world and pushed their sewing machines and knitting baskets deep into their closets.

But today, sewing, knitting, and needlework in general is being reclaimed by women everywhere. Call it the same DIY attitude that saw the rise of riot grrl, or just call it more savvy than paying retail—today's hip chicks are getting busy making sweaters, blankets, cushion covers, and cell phone cozies. Knitting alone has found four million new devotees in the last five years, and the percentage of women under forty-five who knit or crochet has doubled since 1996. Knitting has even been coined "the new yoga," and given its rich history and spiritual benefits, I'd have to say I agree. I'm hooked!

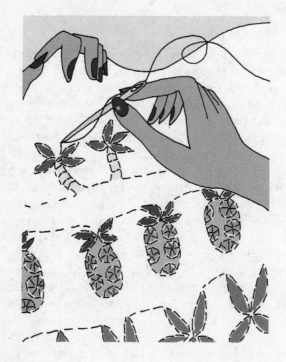

Zen and the art of sewing machine maintenance

Sewing, knitting, embroidering, crocheting—each is a wonderfully meditative experience. How else could these arts have survived the Industrial Revolution, when women no longer had to do them, and still continue to thrive and prosper? Women still choose to do them because they feel so darn good—so naturally Zen.

In many families, the skills, sewing machines, and knitting baskets have been passed down from one generation of women to the next. But not all young women were so lucky—or eager. For those who never learned to sew a hem or knit a bootie, here's an inside tip on the enlightenment of the stitch: there's nothing more nesty than sitting comfortably at home sewing, knitting, or needleworking away an afternoon. But stitching projects do so much more than just make you feel good. If you can master a sewing machine, you can stitch together all kinds of funky threads for your body, not to mention the freshest home furnishings on the block. Whip up a glittery tube top, or a hot dress straight out of an old Bon Jovi video. Hem a long piece of pink satin and sew on fringe for a sex-kitten slipcover, then adorn with a mountain of Thai-inspired silk pillows you made yourself. Stitch together a pleather beanbag chair for friends to sit on, and a cute little vintage-fabric apron to sport while whipping up martinis. Every way you look at it, sewing is a fun, functional, and overall nesty experience—so stitch with it!

Sewing 101

You could hand-stitch all of your projects, but let it be known that hand-stitching is a slow and potentially messy process. Hand-stitched projects generally don't turn out looking as sharp as machine-sewn ones, and they're also less durable. If you do decide to hand-stitch, make sure your measurements are exact, your stitches small and tight, and that you take your sweet time. Hasty hand-stitching may leave you with crooked curtains or an unrecognizable bulk of unraveled fabric on the floor.

If you learn to use a sewing machine, however, chances are better that your end product will turn out looking like you bought it. You'll also find it faster and easier than hand-stitching. The choice is yours. But if you do go the way of the machine, even that dusty one your mother gave you eons ago, here are a few tips to help get you on your way.

✳ Getting a machine. You don't need a machine with every electronic trick switch known to the sewing world, you just need one that fits your skills, your budget, and your apartment. Talk to your local sewing machine dealer. Sometimes you can buy refurbished machines, or even rent them.

✳ Get a book, take a class, go online. There are lots of good learn-to-sew books out there; *Sewing Basics* by Wendy Gardiner is a good one, as is *Sewing for Dummies* by Jan Saunders. The one problem with learning from books is that there's never anyone around to answer your questions—and you will have plenty of questions. On that note, you may want to sign up for a sewing class. Usually classes teach how to use a machine as well as hand-stitching. Call your local fabric store or machine dealer to find classes in your area. Last but not least, you can always go online for a bevy of good, reliable information on sewing. Check out www.sewing.org for online sewing lessons; www.sewingmall.com has a chat room where you can post questions, and www.whatsthebestsewmachine.com will give you the unbiased lowdown on a machine before you plunk down the money to buy it.

Freaky fabric

Every fabric looks, feels, drapes, and sews differently. So what's the best fabric for your project? Here's some information to get you ready for the fabric store. Hint: Always ask about washing instructions; you don't want your sofa slipcover to shrink down to a pillowcase!

Chiffon: A sheer, silky fabric, lovely when draped or layered over a heavier fabric for curtains; or when hung as a room divider.

Cottons/linen: These natural fabrics are soft, durable, easy to sew, and washable. Gingham (two-tone checks), chintz (always with a pattern and glazed up like a doughnut), corduroy, denim, chambray, and canvas (the heavyweight champion) are usually cotton or cotton blends.

Faux fur: Faux fur is fabulous to the touch and doesn't unravel so it never needs to be hemmed, but all that bulk can choke a sewing machine.

Hemp: Hemp is a canvaslike fabric that's harvested from the cannabis plant. It's not as soft as cotton, but it's much stronger (the first Levi's were made of hemp for this very reason).

Pleather: Faux leather and suede are trés chic, and trés today. Think pink pleather pillows or café curtains!

Polyester/rayon/acrylic: These synthetic fabrics can look like natural ones, and they're often cheaper and easier to sew.

Satin: The word "satin" refers to the fabric's shiny finish, not the fabric itself. Satin drapes like liquid, and can look oh-so-romantic.

Silk: Pure silk is a strong, natural fabric that can have a richly textured surface, lovely color gradation, and fabulous drape.

Velvet: Luxuriously soft, but notoriously hard to machine sew.

Go eco

Cotton crops account for half of all pesticides used in the United States. Organic cotton is becoming more popular and easier to find, but if you're serious about going green, you may want to go with hemp. Harvesting hemp is easier on the environment than cotton.

You don't have to be the pink fuzzy slipper and satin-teddy-wearing type to want your nest to have a woman's touch. Be proud of your soft, silky fabrics, lacy trims, and pink shags! The following projects are all fun, easy, and can sugar or spice up your nest, depending on what you want. Use black satin or pink velvet, red pleather or virgin white cotton, soft fringes or faux fur trims—it's up to you. Just take an afternoon, turn on the Sleater-Kinney or Sarah McLachlan, turn off the cell, and give your nest your own special touch. All of these projects can be made with or without a sewing machine.

Silk heart pillows

You can make these out of any fabric you choose, but because they're hearts, sexy fabrics like silk, satin, and velvet look best. You can also spice them up by sewing on a little fringe or racy lace trim!

Get it:

About 1 yard of silk per pillow
1 bag of pillow stuffing
Construction paper

Make it: Cut your favorite heart pattern out of construction paper. Cut the silk into two squares of the same size and pin them together right-side in. Pin the pattern onto the silk, and cut around the paper heart. Using your machine or hand-stitching very carefully, sew the two silk hearts together (still right-side in), leaving at least a ½" seam on the sides, and an unstitched hole 3" long. Now carefully turn the fabric right-side out to hide the hem, push the pillow stuffing through the hole, and then sew the hole closed. Note: If you're adding fringe or lace, sew it along the right-side edge of one of the hearts first, then place it right-side in, and sew the two hearts together.

Fringy three-panel curtains

The three different panels of each of these curtains move separately and allow light to peek through. Mix up the palette by hanging one butter-colored panel sandwiched by two lavender ones, or any color combination you fancy. I like the romanticism of satin, but any fabric works; cotton is clean and crisp, chiffon is sexy and sheer. Sew on beads, plastic butterflies, ribbons, or dried flowers for fabulous flair!

Get it:

About 3 yards total of fabric, one yard for each panel. (Bring
    your window measurements to the fabric store and ask the
    salesperson for help if you need it.)
About 3 yards of fringe
Curtain rod

Make it: Measure the length and width of your windows to determine just how much fabric you need. Add at least 3" in length to allow for the curtain-rod sleeve (depending on the circumference of the rod), and bottom hem; add an inch or two in width to allow for generous window coverage. Cut the fabric into three panels; use a machine or hand-stitch all edges with a ½" seam. Fold fabric over about 1½" on the top and sew a sleeve for the curtain rod. Sew the fringe along the bottom edges of the panels. Hang the panels on the curtain rod, open the windows, and watch them billow in the breeze!

It's "sew you" headboard

If your bed doesn't already have a headboard, why not make one? You can use any type of fabric you choose, but the trick here is to bead it, embroider it, put on mini pom-poms—whatever makes you happy! Remember to do any fabric embellishing before you put it all together.

Get it:

1 piece of plywood about ½" thick, as wide as your bed, as tall
    as you want it to be

1–2 yards of fabric (enough to cover one side of the plywood and wrap around the edges)

1–2 yards of cotton batting (enough to cover one side of the plywood and wrap around the edges)

Screwdriver and three large wood screws (ask your hardware store which ones are best for this project)

Staple gun

Make it: Embellish the fabric any way you want, but keep in mind it will be "hanging" on the wall behind your head. Cover one side of the plywood with cotton batting, using a staple gun to attach the edges to the back of the wood. Place your embellished fabric over the batting, and staple to the back of the plywood. Here's your headboard—now let's attach it. Sit the wood at the head of the bed, butt it up against the wall, and screw it into the wall with three screws across the center. Voila! A padded, personalized headboard!

Racy faux fur rug and pillows

I recommend using faux fur for the rug because it doesn't unravel and doesn't have to be hemmed. However, you could make the pillows with pleather or fake suede for a real rockin' combo.

Rug—Get it:

About 1½ yards of faux fur (depending on how big you want your rug)
Rubber backing (get it at fabric and carpet stores)
Fabric glue
Rug padding (optional)

Make it: You can make your rug any shape you like: round, square, a bone, a heart, whatever! Draw your shape on paper first, pin it to the underside of the faux fur, and cut out the shape. Then glue a good-size piece (or pieces) of rubber backing onto the underside of the fabric, getting it as close to the edges as possible. Lay it on the floor and walk all over it. If it's a little hard on the feet, make it nice and cushy by putting a piece of rug padding under it.

Pillows—Get it:

About I yard of fabric per pillow
I bag of pillow stuffing

Make it: Cut the fabric into two matching pieces. If you're making a funky shape, draw the pattern out on paper first, pin the paper to the two fabric pieces (make sure they're pinned together right-side in), and cut out the shape. Use a machine or hand-stitch the pieces together, leaving a ½" seam around the edges and a 3" hole. Carefully turn the fabric right-side out to hide the hem, stuff, then sew up the hole.

Sex-kitten slipcover

This slipcover is the easiest way to transform any drab old piece of furniture into a fabulous nest piece! Size it to go over a chair or sofa, sew fringes or pompoms on it, or maybe little ribbons or soft satin roses. Imagine a pink or red satin slipcover with gold fringe, dark green velvet with pink satin bows, or a big ol' piece of faux fur. Ooh-la-la!

Get it:

About 3–5 yards of fabric, depending on the size of your chair or sofa
Any adornments you fancy

Make it: To determine how much fabric you'll need, throw a couple of old sheets over your sofa or chair and see which size covers it to your liking. Measure the sheet, and buy a piece of slipcover fabric in the same size. Finish off the edges with a ½" seam all around, and hand-stitch on your adornments of choice. Throw it over your sofa or chair, and tuck it in to give it a nice shape and keep it from slipping off. It's that easy!

Knit wits

Knitting is all the craze these days, and knitting groups known as Stich 'n Bitches are popping up across the country faster than Star-

bucks. It seems everybody's got needle fever, and hand-knit bags, doggie booties, and cell phone holders are all the rage. Never tried your hand at knitting but have a hankering to learn? You won't find the how-tos here; that's enough information to fill another book—or books. But I can help point you in the right direction. *Stitch 'n Bitch* by Debbie Stoller is a great book for beginners; it will have you knitting and purling in no time at all. For you more advanced knit wits, *Weekend Knitting* by Melanie Falick and *Simple Knits for Sophisticated Living* by Barbara Albright offer plenty of fresh insights and funky patterns.

If the books just aren't doing it for you, why not take a knitting class and get support from like-minded girls who're just as confused as you are? Call them a prerequisite to a Stitch 'n Bitch, knitting classes are informative, fun, and you're sure to make new friends. Call your local yarn stores to find the best classes for a knitter of your caliber.

Hollywood knitters

Contrary to popular belief, the hottest trend to hit Tinseltown isn't Atkins, Pilates, or even dating younger men—it's knitting. It seems that many stars are finding things to do in between takes other than just learning their lines—they're picking up the knitting sticks and creating fabulous scarves, blankets, and sweaters. Who's the who of celebrity knitters? The lovely Jennifer Beals knit Steven Tyler of Aerosmith an eight-foot-long red chenille scarf; the charming Lauren Ambrose learned to knit on the set of *Six Feet Under*; Debra Messing, Cameron Diaz, Sarah Jessica Parker, Madonna, and indie "it" girl Parker Posey are all knit wits; and Daryl Hannah has gone on record to say that knitting is meditative and calming.

Other great resources for beginners are family and friends who knit. Knitters are a tight bunch, and if you express an interest and reach out, someone is sure to take you by the hand. Who knows? You may even inherit a starter bag full of needles and yarn!

Here are just a few of the more nesty items you and your needles can create; most of these patterns are available for free on the Internet, just search "knitting patterns."

* Sofa covers
* Pillow shams
* Dishcloths
* Hanger covers
* Tissue-box covers
* Aprons
* Table runners
* Tea cozies
* Slippers
* Pet pillows
* Ottoman covers
* Pot holders
* Sachets
* Toilet paper covers
* Cell phone cozies

Knit online

Do you toss and turn at night thinking about that unfinished afghan? Do your friends think you've lost it because all you talk about is yarn gauge? Need a baby bootie pattern pronto? Don't fret, just hop online and join the millions of hip young women chatting and dishing about their knitting addiction. Here are a few of the better-known knitting sites, and there are plenty more where these came from. Just log on and knit on!

Knitty.com   Knitting.about.com
Knitlist.com   Knitpicks.com

Yarn it!

Before you start any knitting project, you'll need to know your yarn. There are more textures, qualities, and weights of yarn than you can shake your needles at, but here's a basic rundown of your choices:

Acrylic: On the upside, acrylic is cheap and washes very nicely. On the downside, it isn't as soft or luxurious as natural yarns, and it's a pesky petroleum product.

Angora: Soft as a bunny because it comes from a bunny. But because it sheds like a bunny, angora may not be the best yarn choice save for accents.

Cashmere: Combed from the bellies of goats, "cash"-mere is oh-so-expensive but oh-so-luxurious. A less expensive alternative is a cashmere yarn with wool woven in with it.

Mohair: A shaggy, fuzzy goat wool. Mohair has a soft, chic look and makes for great lap blankets, scarves, and ottoman covers, but it can be itchy all the same.

Wool: Sheep's wool is warm but usually scratchy. You may want to use Merino wool, as it's soft and sweet against the skin. Perfect for a warm, snuggly blanket.

Felting up

Remember that baggy wool sweater that went through the wash and came out sized to fit your baby nephew? That's the science behind felting, a super-hip knitting trick. In order to felt an item, you use a special felting pattern (you knit it too big because it's going to shrink), wool yarn, large needles, and simple stitches. Once the item is knit, you purposely throw it into a hot washing machine and it shrinks up into a thickly textured masterpiece that fits you perfectly! Because the item loses so much stitch detail, the stitches for felting patterns are very basic—fabulous for knitting novices!

Tips

- Thicker needles produce more open, airy fabric (good for sweaters), while smaller needles knit a tighter one (good for dishcloths).

- A purl stitch is nothing but a backward knit stitch. When you knit, you pull the loop from the back to the front of the old loop; and when you purl, you push the loop through the front to the back of the old loop.

- When knitting sweaters for the family, don't forget your fuzzy buddies! Go to www.thedietdiary.com/cgi-bin/chart_dog.pl, and get the instructions you need to knit a custom-fitted dog or cat sweater.

Did you know?

According to a 2000 survey by the Craft Yarn Council, one in three women is getting busy with her knitting sticks!

Scrapbooking

You know you have them. The shoe boxes upon shoe boxes stuffed with old fading photos, memorabilia, and other records of good times you just can't bear to throw away. The skate-rental ticket from your sweet sixteen roller-skating party. The senior prom picture with your big hair, disastrous dress, and even more disastrous date (what was his name?). The black-and-white photos of your grandparents when they were eighteen and in love. Or the concert stubs from Cher's Final Tour 1988, 2000, and 2002.

You've kept all of this stuff because you knew that someday you'd want to dust it off, share it, and reminisce. I mean, who would ever believe you held a backstage pass to a Nirvana concert? Or that your hunky brother sported an afro and headgear in the sixth grade? Or that your mom wore army boots? Some photos and items are just too precious to part with, but now that you've kept them—what the heck are you supposed to do with them?

What is scrapbooking?

Scrapbooking is exactly what it sounds like: sitting down for an afternoon here and there and arranging your old photos and memorabilia into scrapbooks. We're not talking about the documentary-style photo albums your mom used to keep—modern-day scrapbooking is so much more than placing photos in straight rows under yellowing plastic sheets in self-stick photo albums. It's getting busy with colored pens and card stocks, die cuts, funky fabrics, stencils, stickers, decorative-edged scissors and rulers, lettering kits, watercolors, rubber stamps, and patina paints. It's the oh-so-artful act of arranging, decorating, journaling, and personalizing a scrapbook that's fun, funky, and so you!

Scrapbooking stores, magazines, Web sites, and clubs are popping up left and right. So what's all the fuss about, anyway? How can the job of rifling through stacks upon stacks of unorganized photos, playbills, and pressed flowers ever possibly be something you'd volunteer to do on a free afternoon, much less end up being something you actually enjoy doing? It's all in how you go about it.

Scrappin' made simple

Photos and memorabilia can get ruined and mysteriously disappear with time, as can your memory. When you scrapbook, you're documenting names, dates, places and events while they're still in your head, or at least it's incentive enough to get on the horn and ask your friends if they remember. It's a fun, effective way to keep the good times alive.

But scrapbooking can also be a bit intimidating. The piles upon piles of memorabilia can present themselves as a project with no end. But if you organize and tackle the project one bite at a time, you'll find you can actually sit back on a leisurely Sunday afternoon, turn on the music, and have a blast browsing through all your old stuff.

Get the party started

So you're ready to give scrapbooking a try. Bravo! But don't pick up the glue sticks and glitter quite yet. Getting started is the most important part, and a proper plan of attack is needed to ensure you finish what you start. Here's a step-by-step plan to help you breeze through the most difficult part of the scrapbooking process—the organizing of the photos and other memorabilia.

The big "O"

Put on the Marvin Gaye and slip into something more comfortable, ladies, it's time to get organized. It doesn't have to be as time-consuming as you might think, although if you decide to organize everything you've got, it could take an entire afternoon or two, depending on the size and state of your stash. But even if it does take a whole rainy weekend, there's nobody saying you can't uncork a bottle of red and make a good time of it. For those in a time pinch, you can start by just scrapbooking one or two rolls of film, but all of those old photos need to be organized at some point, right? There's no better time than the present.

1. Make space: Clear a table, the couch, or a spot on the floor. Bottom line is you want to be comfortable and have plenty of space to spread out.

2. Box it up: Assemble a collection of small- to medium-sized boxes. You'll want one box for each member of your family, and a stash of on-call boxes that you'll designate for photographs of certain events, like your parents' anniversary, or your most recent wine-tasting party. You'll also want at least one box for memorabilia: dried prom corsages, old drawings, love letters; one box for mystery items that you'll want to call Mom or friends about in order to ID or date; and a box for garbage: photos with heads cut off, things that are too faded to read any longer, and memorabilia that doesn't make the cut. Label each box accordingly.

3. Write it up: Start going through your stuff and putting photos into their appropriate boxes, but don't box it until you've labeled it! You'll want to use a photo-labeling pencil (available at crafts stores), as these waxy pencils let you write on photos and then wipe it off later. Other pens may cause indents or even bleed through your photos, so do take care. Label the photos with names, events, dates, and any blurbs you want to call out. For memorabilia, tape, tie, or stick on notes with the appropriate info, then put them in their designated boxes.

4. Wrap it up: Once you have all of your photos and memories neatly organized into their own boxes, congratulate yourself. You've tackled the most tedious and time-consuming part of scrapbooking, and even if some of those photos never make it onto a scrapbook page, at least you have them all categorized and documented.

Red-eye

Don't let a little dose of red-eye ruin a perfect photo. Get a red-eye pen at the craft store. They contain a dye that filters out the red, changing your fiery glare back into a cool, baby blue.

Drop the acid

You know that old, yellow, brittle scrapbook in your parents' attic? That's your scrapbook on acid, in twenty years. The good news is that most craft stores and almost all scrapbooking stores are privy to the effects of acid and offer a fabulous array of acid-free albums, papers, glues, pens, cards, stickers, and photo corners. Ask before you buy.

Top ten tools

Check the Yellow Pages or go to www.creatingkeepsakes.com to see if there's a scrapbooking store in your area, as they'll undoubtedly have the best selection of supplies and knowledge to dish out. If your 'hood doesn't host a scrapbooking store, you can buy online (see page 90), or just go to your local craft stores and hunt down the following items.

1. Scrapbook: You can use a photo album, three-ring binder, or bound scrapbook, but keep in mind that three-ring binders and any expandable binding will allow you to add and remove pages any time you want, which is a bonus. Choose a book that allows the pages to lie flat, and a size that fits your project. In other words, if you're making a scrapbook of all the men you've loved before, you may want to get a book that can hold a lot of pages! If the book has a cover that you like, that's great, but you can always create your own cover (see the Cover it up section on page 90.)

2. Adhesives: Whether you go with glue sticks, mounting tape, pastes, or liquid glue pens, always make sure it's photo-safe.

Some adhesives, like rubber cement and cellophane tape, actually destroy photos over time.

3. **Card stock:** Card stock's thick, durable pages are best for scrapbooks, and it comes in hundreds of colors and weights. Heavier-weight card stocks are used as the ground paper, the paper that everything is mounted on. Lighter-weight stocks are what you cut up into a million different funky shapes and glue all over the pages, on top of the heavier paper.

4. **Scissors:** You'll want one pair of small, sharp, straight-edged scissors, but you should also explore the wonderful world of decorative scissors: squiggly lines, sharp points, waves. Get a whole kit and really party down.

5. **Pens:** You'll want to write on your scrapbook pages to document names, dates, and places, and to dish any inside stories. Colored pencils, calligraphy pens, feathers dipped in ink, metallic pens . . . again, the choice is yours. But make sure whatever you choose is permanent, fade-proof, and waterproof. Also be sure to pick up that photo-labeling pencil while you're in the store.

6. **Photo corners:** These allow you to mount your photos with minimal adhesive, and they have a fabulous timeless appeal to boot. They come in all different colors and patterns, from simple to super fancy.

7. **Templates/stencils:** Templates and stencils can help you cut photos and paper into cool shapes like hearts, stars, or diamonds.

8. **Lettering books:** They come filled with all styles of letters that you can trace onto your scrapbook pages. They make your headers and writing look almost pro!

9. **Party favors:** Get it on with stickers, die cuts (precut paper shapes), punches (to punch out cool paper shapes), rubber stamps, tinfoil, beads, macaroni, appliqués, and vintage fabrics. You can glue just about anything to your pages with a hot glue gun, including your memorabilia, such as ticket stubs, pressed flowers, and old valentines!

10. Sheet protectors: You may want to protect your masterpiece pages from fingerprints and other mishaps by putting them in protective plastic sleeves. Both Mylar and the cheaper polypropylene pages have been deemed safe for scrapbooking.

What's your story?

Scrapbooking is all about telling a story. You gather your photos, memorabilia, and words, and display them on a page so that when the book is opened, your story is told again and again. How to best tell your story? That's your call. Just as the same story can be told a hundred different ways, the same scrapbook page can be displayed a hundred different ways.

If you're new to this, I highly recommend browsing through a scrapbooking Web site, magazine, or book (see page 90), and perusing the cornucopia of photo, layout, and decorating techniques. There are so many different ideas, we could never go over all of them here, but the following is an introduction to some of the more popular techniques and tricks.

Pick a pic

The first thing you want to do is select a topic or theme for your page. To make things easy, let's pretend you've chosen a theme of spring break in Maui. Now select two to four photographs that relay the story you want the page to tell. Mix the photo subjects and styles for interest; you don't want four photos of the same sunset taken in one-minute intervals (yawn). Maybe start by choosing a photo of the overall "scene" (your beach towels, lotion bottles, and margarita glasses); an activity shot (burying each other in the sand); a funny moment (a stray dog running off with your bikini top), and a personal close-up of the entire group at sunset.

Once you've chosen the photos to tell your story, start thinking about other things you might want to glue or write down on the page. Maybe write about how you had to sneak onto the beach because it was private; or gluing down the friendship bracelets you all bought, a few seashells, or margarita-glass-shaped die cuts. Now that's the way to tell a good story!

Layout tips

Page layout is where most people get a little stressed. People assume that layout is something only professional designers know how to do, but they're wrong. Layouts generally follow very simple, basic rules, like how placing photos horizontally will give you a clean look, while placing them at an angle will create more interest. Here are a few tips to help you get started.

Triangle trick: Take the three largest items (photos or memorabilia), and put them in a triangle pattern anywhere on the page (if you were to connect the photos with a pencil, you would draw a triangle). The triangle layout keeps everything balanced.

Magazines: Your magazine rack is a great place to search for a workable layout. Every page in every magazine has a layout; just find one that works for you and copy it. An excellent place to view scrapbook-specific layouts is in a scrapbooking magazine (see page 90).

Web sites: Visit any of the Web sites listed on page 90. Many of them have lots of fresh scrapbook layouts you can peruse for a dose of design inspiration.

Mind your header: When designing a page's layout, don't forget to leave space for your header. A header is the title theme for a page, like "High School Hotties" or "My First Turkey Day Dinner." You can design it any way you please, with the header on top, along the bottom, or stacked from top to bottom, but it should have a fairly prominent piece of your page's real estate. Of course, your page doesn't have to have a header, but it does help tie everything together.

Negative space: When it comes to your pages, there can be such a thing as too much stuff. You may want to set some space aside for nothing at all. This "negative space" will give your eyes a place to rest on the page, cut down on the clutter, and make your important items stand out more.

Find a focus: You always want one main focal point per page. It gives your eye a place to start. You can make any item a focal point by making it bigger than everything else, or more colorful, or more glittery—just make it stand out!

Lay it down

Once you've sketched out a basic layout, it's time to start putting everything down on your ground paper. But just like every other step of scrapbooking, there's an order to laying your photos and objects on the page. The trick is to start big and finish small. That way, you're sure to get all the important stuff down first, and you can just keep adding embellishments until you're happy. Here's a basic idea of how to go about gluing everything down.

1. Ground paper: This is the background for your entire page, so choose a color that fits the theme or mood you want to convey. Ground paper with a pattern will always spice things up a bit.

2. Photos: Cut out a piece of card stock ¼" bigger than your photo on all sides and glue your photo to it for an instant frame (decorative scissors help make unique photo frames!). Use a template and cut your photos into circle, diamond, or star shapes. Try scanning your photos and printing some out as black and white to add something different to an otherwise colorful page.

3. Header: Once the photos are glued down, it's time to write your header, or title. Get out your lettering booklet and get busy tracing; or create it on the computer; or just get the calligraphy pen and freehand it. You can draw or print your header on one piece of paper, cut it into a funky shape, and then layer it over another piece of paper; write it on a piece of card stock that's trimmed with lace or faux fur; or buy the letters as die cuts and layer them on top of the photos—just have

fun with it! This is also the time when you'll want to write down any funny stories, or names and dates, etc.

4. **Embellishments:** Now that the three basic design elements are in place, it's time to turn it up a notch. Get creative with the decorative scissors, colorful card stocks, colored pens, and die cuts. Now's the time to punch out those tinfoil stars, glue down those dried petals from your prom corsage, play with those stickers, and make the page sparkle with pink glitter.

5. **Page protectors:** Once you have the page looking just as you like it, let it dry overnight, then slip it into a page protector and into your scrapbook. Show off the book to friends and family every chance you get.

DIY ground paper

Scan your favorite vintage dress, barrettes, gummy bears, or Chinese matchboxes; then print the image out on card stock for customized ground paper! If your printer can't handle card stock, Kinko's can print it out for you. You can also tea-stain card stock for a vintage look (see page 22 for technique).

Tips

■ Just as your page has a story theme, it's nice for it to have a color theme, too. An Oscar-night party theme might translate best with lavish golds and silvers; a family picnic might be fitting for reds, whites, and checks; and a rock 'n' roll slumber party might see a lot of red, black, and zebra print.

■ If you want to enlarge, cut, or crop one-of-a-kind or old family photos, consider scanning them and printing them out on photo paper rather than altering the originals.

■ Adobe Photoshop is a great computer software program that allows you to manipulate your photos any way you want. Just scan the image, and then you can enlarge it, distort it, color it, weather it, even add and delete objects.

Cover it up

After spending all this time designing, drawing, gluing, and embellishing the inside of your scrapbook, don't forget to give the outside some love as well.

You can buy a scrapbook with a fancy, premade cover, but it's so much more fun to trick it out yourself. Cover it with vintage fabric and fresh appliqués or iron-ons, or a piece of denim from a pair of old jeans; or faux fur; or a piece of your Wonder Woman pillowcases. If your scrapbook has a specific theme, like travel, think about covering it with a map, or make you own cover by scanning money, stamps, or postcards from around the world, or your passport pages.

Where the scrappers are

The following Web sites and magazines offer a wealth of information and inspiration. Whether you're looking for a scrapbooking store, want to start up a club or take a class, are hunting for supplies, or just want to find a good layout to steal—look here first.

Magazines

* *Creating Keepsakes* (www.creatingkeepsakes.com)
* *Memory Makers* (www.memorymakersmagazine.com)
* *Simple Scrapbook* (www.simplescrapbooksmag.com)
* *PaperKuts* (www.paperkuts.com)

Web sites

* www.scrapbooking.com
* www.scrappinfools.com
* www.gonescrappin.com
* www.scrapbookingtop50.com

Journaling

If you want to preserve memories but aren't quite motivated enough to scrapbook, keeping a journal is a great way to chronicle the days (and nights!) of your life and spend quality time alone in your nest. Journaling is very therapeutic and can even help you work out personal problems. Visit your local book or crafts store to find a journal that strikes you. A prestigious leather-bound journal will last forever; a journal covered in Indian fabric is exotic and colorful; a sketch book is artsy; and a college-ruled spiral notebook casual and familiar. Set aside a specific time each day (before you go to bed may be best), and spill your story. Write down whatever comes to mind, no matter how silly or cruel, embarrassing or sad, long or short. Express your thoughts any way you want—as stories, poems, sketches, haiku, whatever. Some days you might write five pages, some days five words; it doesn't matter. The only thing that matters is that you tell it like it is, and tell yourself the truth.

Let It Grow

● ●

Plants are truly fabulous. They give us the air we breathe, the food we eat, the shade we seek, and the medicine we need. But in to-day's concrete jungles, where parking lots have replaced flower fields and skyscrapers have outgrown forests, it's easy to forget about the plant world and the healing, calming, grounding effect it has on our everyday lives. All the more reason to bring plants into our homes, I say.

Every nest can benefit from the nurturing touches of something green. Giving your time and patience to an indoor herb garden is a calming, ever-so-nesty experience that rewards you with herbal in-fusions, savory seasoning oils, and fresh flavor for your sauces every night of the week. Small pots of lavender and rosemary will make your nest look cozy and smell like a spa. Talking to and nurturing your hanging ferns and gerbera daisies is not only therapeutic, but the plants remove toxins from the air so you breathe easier and healthier. Yes, plants are amazing, and the following section is all about learning how to bring them into your home so that you can enjoy their healthy green mojo every day. Even if you haven't had much luck with plants in the past, it's time to turn over a new leaf. Get your potting soil and watering cans ready, ladies. We're going green.

Herbal history

Herbs have been used for medicinal purposes since the begin-ning of civilization as we know it. As far back as 2500 BC, the Assyrians carved inscriptions onto clay tablets documenting the healing powers of herbs. Around 1500 BC, the Indian Vedas spoke of the magical powers of these aromatic little plants. But all this medicinal history aside, when was it that somebody first discovered that fresh basil tastes fabulous with a slice of fresh tomato and mozzarella? Or that chopped mint leaves zest up any salad? Or that rosemary roasted potatoes are simply to die for?

Herbs are not only good for you, they taste fabulous. For the avid cook, fresh herbs are a culinary necessity, and there's nothing like reaching over into your own garden and picking a few succulent leaves to instantly add a burst of fresh flavor to any dish. So you love the idea of fresh herbs, the look of them, the smell of them, the taste of them, but you don't have a backyard or garden to grow them in? No worries! Many herbs grow quite nicely indoors. As long as you have a sunny window (or even artificial indoor lights will do), a little potting soil, good containers, and a lot of patience—you have what it takes to grow an indoor herb garden.

What grows?

Which herbs do you want to grow? Do you want the herbs for your salads and sauces, for making your own aromatherapy oils (see page 55), or just for the ambience of having plants in the house? Think about it. Also think about how much time you want to spend on your plants. If you're a girl on the go with only an evening here and a Saturday afternoon there to spend with your garden, don't grow twenty different herbs right off the bat—you won't have enough love to give to all of them. As a rule, start small and let your garden grow from there.

Some herbs do better indoors than others. Here's a list of some delectable herbs that are generally easier to grow indoors:

* Basil: Green sweet basil, purple basil, Japanese basil, lemon basil—there are more types of basil than you can shake a leaf at, and they're all peppery, sweet, and great for making stir fries and pesto.

* Chives: Chives are a great starter herb because they're so easy to grow indoors. Delicious on baked potatoes, with fish, and in breads; chives are packed with vitamins A and C.
* Dill: Don't start those homemade pickles without it! Dill is easy to grow and also delicious sprinkled on salmon and mixed in with cream cheese, butter, and sour cream for a fabulous baked potato topper.
* Lemon balm: This refreshing, minty herb is easy to grow indoors and refreshing as a tea infusion and in salads.
* Mint: Most people grow spearmint and the stronger peppermint, but all mint is good for digestion and delicious in iced tea, salads, and frosty mint juleps!
* Oregano: A must for any fresh tomato sauce, oregano is also delicious with eggs, beans, and potatoes.
* Parsley: Packed with vitamins and minerals, parsley is the main flavor in tabbouleh and makes a nice garnish to boot.
* Rosemary: A bit more difficult to grow indoors than the others listed here, but well worth it. Rosemary is delectable with meat and in breads, and as a cooking and aromatherapy oil.
* Tarragon: The aromatic and tasty French tarragon is what you want; Russian tarragon can taste a bit like grass. A must in homemade hollandaise and tarter sauces!
* Winter savory: A peppery mix between mint and thyme, winter savory is a good complement to beans of all kinds, whether they're in hot soups or cold salads.

What a plant wants

You want to grow healthy, tasty, aromatic plants, but in order for this to happen, there are some basic rules that you need to follow. Herbs and all indoor plants are very finicky, and if they don't like their living situation, they'll just get angry and die on you. Even if they do like their living situation, sometimes they decide to die on you anyway. You have to be patient, and learn as you grow.

Here's a rundown of the basic necessities most indoor herbs (and plants) need in order to grow strong and healthy. Every plant's needs are different, and you should always research the particular plant you're trying to grow, but these basics always come into play, whether you're planting purple basil or a Boston fern.

1. A good start

Starting plants from seeds is a difficult process; you're probably better off going to your local nursery and bringing home a starter plant you can start harvesting right away! Call nurseries in your area to see what starter plants they have in stock—you might have to ask that they start a particular plant for you if they don't usually carry it.

2. A good home

An indoor plant needs a home—a container to grow in. The two most important things to remember when choosing a container are (1) to make sure it's big enough; for a single herb plant, you'll want a pot at least eight to ten inches in diameter; and (2) that it has good drainage. With that in mind, you can pot a plant in just about anything you fancy.

If you go down to your local nursery or garden center, you'll see stacks upon stacks of clay and plastic containers, good potential homes for your herbs. Clay containers are prettier to look at, and unlike unbreathable plastic pots they're porous and help control the moisture of the soil. Do keep in mind that you'll need to soak a clay pot in water before you plant in it, otherwise it will suck the water right out of your soil!

It's all about drainage

A plant needs drainage, otherwise it drowns. Whether or not your container has a drainage hole, always line the bottom with at least 2" of pebbles, sand, or small pieces from a broken clay pot. Then pour in your potting soil. If your container doesn't have drainage holes, just punch them yourself; if this is impossible, increase the thickness of the drainage material at the bottom of the container.

Try rummaging through your nest or go thrift shopping to find some fun, funky, unexpected plant containers. Herbs look fabulous in just about anything that looks weathered or vintage. Imagine your garden growing in old olive oil containers, galvanized steel boxes, chipped cookie jars, vintage soup bowls, metal watering cans, bright beach buckets, even an old cowboy boot!

DIY containers: Terra cotta pots are rustic but suck moisture from your soil; bamboo pots are chic but can split; dyed concrete pots are modern but not waterproof; glass pots are sleek but usually offer no drainage; iron pots may rust; and plastic pots are cheap. The choices of planting containers are plentiful nowadays, and as long as you know the pros and cons of your container, you can find a pot that both looks cool and lets your plant thrive. But why not customize a pot especially for your nest? Here are a few ideas.

* Take a terra cotta pot and spray paint it a sleek silver or gold, or first paint on a white base coat and then add bright, preppy stripes; maybe paint your version of a Matisse, or colorwash it white for a beachy look.
* Put any plastic pot in a bigger glass container, then fill in the space with sea glass, shells, or stones until you can't see the plastic.
* Take any pot and tie twigs, painted popsicle sticks, bamboo, or anything long and tall around the outside, or wrap a string of lights around it.
* Use a glue gun to attach glass beads, vintage buttons, plastic fireflies, or any other favorite paraphernalia around the outside of any pot.

3. The good earth

You've got a perky little starter plant and a cool container to put it in. Now you need to plant it in the good old earth. But not all dirt is created equal. The most reliable way to get a good pot of dirt is to go to your local nursery or gardening center and buy a bag of high-quality potting mix. Tell the sales associate what you'll be growing, and they may even be able to recommend a specific brand or mix to help you out. Never go to the park or into your backyard and grab a handful of dirt to throw in your pot. It probably has weed seeds, and may not be suitable for growing.

4. Compost happens

No matter how rich the earth you plant in, your soil is going to need a little food, or fertilizer, from time to time. Fertilizer is the organic matter that feeds the microorganisms that feed the soil that in turn feeds your herbs. Got it? Now get it.

You can buy premade organic or nonorganic fertilizer while you're at the nursery, but don't necessarily follow the instructions on the bag. Indoor plants grow more slowly than outdoor ones and need less fertilizer, so you'll probably want to use about half the recommended amount. Talk to an expert at the nursery.

You can also try your hand at making your own fertilizer, otherwise known as composting. As my grandma used to say, there's no better fertilizer than the stuff that comes out of your own kitchen! Put a coffee can next to the sink and use it to store used espresso grounds, eggshells, veggie and fruit scraps, leftover sushi seaweed, and leaves that fall off your plants. Just mix it in with your soil once a month or as needed, and watch your plants grow!

Tip: Nonorganic (or synthetic) fertilizers are more of a quick fix, not a long-term solution. They'll give your plants a quick boost of nutrition, but they won't do much to feed the soil.

5. Lighten up

When it comes to light, you want to give your indoor plants the same light they would receive if they were outside. Keep plants by windows, and remember to open the blinds when you get up in the morning. As plants grow toward the light, turn them every so often so they don't grow crooked. But do be careful with your light. Plants can sizzle on sills in the summer months, and freeze to windows in the winter, so make sure your plants are getting just what they need, not too much, not too little. One advantage to indoor gardening is that if a plant needs more light or a warmer spot, you can simply pick it up and move it!

If you're opening the blinds every morning at the crack of dawn and moving your plants from sunny spot to sunny spot, and they're still crying for more light—it may be time to think about artificial lighting. Go to the hardware store and buy a hanging or clip-on lamp with a hood to direct the light down onto the plant. As far as bulbs go, you can spend the money on special grow bulbs, but fluorescents are cheap and work just as well. Hang the light about a foot away from your plants, and shine it on your plants anywhere from fourteen to sixteen hours a day. You might want to buy a light timer while you're at the hardware store so that you don't have to remember to turn the lamp on and off every day.

Tip: Hang a sheer curtain in your window and give your delicate plant all the sunlight it wants without the intensity.

6. Watering can

Everybody knows plants need to be watered, but did you know that many indoor plants get too much of the stuff? Indoor plants tend to need less water than outdoor plants. Watering once a week is a good idea, but keen observation is an even better one. Instead of just mindlessly watering every week, dip your finger in the soil first. If the top is dry, give it a little drink. Otherwise, move on to the next plant. Keep in mind that if your herbs are in plastic or any non-porous pots, they'll need less water than if they're in clay pots; and if you keep your thermostat cranked, or if your radiator pumps out the extra-dry heat, it's best to check the water level twice a week.

Tips

- How would you like it if someone poured cold water over your head? Plants don't like it either. Give them tepid water instead of a cold shower.

- Plants love to have their leaves misted. Give them a soft tepid-water misting twice a week and see their leaves glow.

- Plants love wet, humid areas like greenhouses—and bathrooms! Move plants into the bathroom with you once a week and take a steamy bath. Your plants will love it, and so will you!

---

7. Love and Zen

Perhaps the most important thing to remember when growing your indoor garden is that plants, like people, need love and attention. You can't just plant the little starters in their pots, put them in a sunny corner, and expect them to start pumping out tasty leaves at will. Plants are very sensitive creatures. They need to be coerced into blooming, they need to be guided toward the light, and they need to be nurtured to good health.

You need to spend time with your herbs, and all your indoor plants for that matter, cutting off leaves that have wilted, moving pots around to sunnier spots, misting, and checking soil. While all this responsibility may sound unappealing, it's exactly this plant–person interaction that makes the whole growing experience so rewarding. If you care enough to take one morning a week to nurture and pamper and water and preen, not only will you find the entire experience very Zen and therapeutic, but your plants just may reward you with their most delicious bounty!

You grow, girl!

If you ever have any questions about seed starting, flower-part naming, compost making, or anything plant related, be sure to visit www.yougrowgirl.com. It's by far the best online forum for the urban gardener. With DIY attitude and hip, herbicide-free insight, it's chock-full of useful information, tips, forums, and even art. Be sure to check out the fabulous "garden hoe" Ts in the store!

Let's eat!

So, you've planted and watered and told your herbs your deepest, darkest secrets, and now some of them are looking good enough to eat. Let's take an afternoon, meander into the kitchen, and enjoy the fruits of your labor—let's eat your herbs! If you're having a hard time picking those lovely green leaves you've mothered for so long, don't worry—more will grow in their place!

Hip herb vinegar or oil

Get it:

Herbs of choice
rice wine or red wine vinegar **or** olive oil (enough to fill whatever
   bottle, jar, or container you choose)

Make it: Take a handful of herbs and smash them a bit with a mortar and
pestle or a rolling pin to release their oils. Put them in a glass bottle, and
add your vinegar or oil. Put the bottle in a warm place, let stand for at least
two weeks, then strain out the old herbs and add a few fresh sprigs to make
it look professional. Flavored vinegars and oils are wonderful for cooking,
look fabulous lined up on a kitchen shelf, and make great gifts!

Heavenly herb butter or cream cheese

Get it:

I cup soft butter or cream   I cup herbs of choice
   cheese

Make it: You can either chop the herbs by hand and just mix them in
with the butter or cream cheese, or put everything in a blender—both
ways work just fine. Add a little pepper, parmesan, or Tabasco and really
turn it up a notch!

Delectable herb mustard

Get it:

   White wine vinegar   Salt
I cup dry mustard powder   Herbs of your choice, finely
   Sugar   chopped

Make it: Pour the vinegar into the mustard powder and mix until you get a nice paste. Add sugar and salt to taste. For the final touch, add some of those homegrown herbs. Great on sandwiches, or put it in beautiful jars and give as gifts!

To-drool-for pesto

Get it:

- 4 cups basil leaves
- 4 cloves garlic
- ¾ cup olive oil
- ½–1 cup freshly grated parmesan
- More olive oil

Make it: Put basil and garlic in a blender, pour in the ¾ cup olive oil, and blend until smooth. Pour mixture into a bowl, stir in cheese to taste, and slowly add more oil until you're happy with the consistency. Boil some fresh pasta and call your friends! (Note: you can freeze pesto, but do it before you add the cheese and extra oil.)

Crispy dill cucumbers

Get it:

- 4 cucumbers
- 1 tablespoon salt
- ⅓ cup sugar
- ⅓ cup white vinegar
- 1 tablespoon chopped dill leaves

Make it: Peel and cut cucumbers into very thin slices (a potato peeler works wonders). Put in a shallow pan, add salt, cover with cold water, and put in the fridge for several hours. Combine sugar and vinegar in another small pan and slowly heat on the stove until the sugar dissolves. Add the dill leaves and cool. Drain and rinse the cucumbers. Pour the vinegar mixture over the cucumbers, and chill until you're ready to eat this crispy, zingy snack. So refreshing on a hot summer day!

Mushroom caps

Get it:

½ pound fresh white
  mushrooms, destemmed
I lemon
½ pound small white onions,
  diced

¾ cup olive oil
¼ cup vinegar
I clove minced garlic
¼ cup chopped oregano

Make it: Place mushrooms in a saucepan and squeeze the lemon over them. Peel onions, add them to saucepan, cover with water, and bring to a boil. Turn down the heat and simmer for five minutes. Drain, then toss in a bowl with remaining ingredients. Let marinate at room temperature for at least three hours, and enjoy! (For even more flavor, marinate the whole shebang in the fridge for several days, but bring it all back to room temperature before you gobble it up.)

Middle Eastern tabbouleh

Get it:

I cup dry bulgur (cracked wheat)
2½ cups parsley
½ cup mint leaves
I cup chopped chives
  or scallions

½ cup lemon juice
½ cup olive oil
I tomato
I cucumber
Salt and pepper

Make it: Put bulgur in a large bowl, cover with water, and let soak until soft (about an hour). Drain, then spread out on a cloth or paper towel to absorb excess moisture. Blend parsley, mint, chives or scallions, lemon juice, and oil in a blender. Put the bulgur back into a bowl and add the blended herbal mixture and finely chopped tomato and cucumber. Sprinkle in salt and pepper to taste, and you have tabbouleh. Serve with pita bread, and wow your belly-dancing class!

Beyond herbs

Herbs are tasty, fragrant, and look so cute in their little pots, but they're just the beginning of the indoor planting opportunities that await you. You can take all the growing tips from the herb section and apply them to the hundreds of plants that you can grow, nurture, and benefit from in your very own nest. Houseplants may not give you the culinary satisfaction that herbs do, but did you know that they remove unwanted toxins and pollutants from your breathing space, as well as add moisture to the air and create a calming, grounding environment? It's true. Houseplants are a beautiful, colorful, healthy addition to any nest—especially yours.

Be on top of it

Whether you're growing oregano or orchids, always think about what you're going to put on the surface of your potting soil. If you leave just plain soil on top, aside from being boring to look at, the dirt will also inevitably end up on your table. Think about lightly placing moss, broken seashells, pebbles, smooth stones, agates, or sea glass on top of it all. It'll make your plants look that much more fabulous, and keep your tables clean!

Hip houseplants

Plants are the ultimate interior design accessory. They add a splash of warming green to an otherwise sterile, white room; they soften sharp corners with their curvy, fragrant leaves. A cacti collection polishes off a southwestern theme; a window box of gerbera daisies livens up a chrome kitchen; a lush fern looks fabulous against a coral colorwashed wall. The possibilities are endless, and you should treat houseplants the same way you would treat your curtains, paint colors, and room accessories—they're a part of the bigger picture. Whether your style is a sharp, minimalist agave plant or an African blushing philodendron, a sexy orchid or a natural beach grass, there's a plant with the perfect color, texture, shape, and fragrance to complement every room in your nest. Go to your local nursery and have a look around. Think outside the pot!

Breathe easy

While you're reading this, you're probably breathing in small amounts of formaldehyde, ammonia, xylene, toluene, mold spores, and other chemicals. But you're sitting inside, you say? Safe from the outdoor smog? This may come as a bit of a surprise, but it's because you're indoors that you're breathing in these harmful chemicals.

The Environmental Protection Agency has stated that indoor air can be up to 80 percent more polluted than outdoor air. Paint, cleaning products, nail polish remover, permanent press clothes, tissue paper, carpet, furniture, garbage bags, plywood, gas stoves—all of these common household products release noxious chemicals and toxins into the air. Considering the average American spends 90 percent of his or her life inside, indoor pollution is a hot topic and a growing health concern. It's already been linked to Sick Building Syndrome (SBS), allergies, asthma, fatigue, headache, nervous system disorders, and even some cancers. So what can you do? You can be more conscious of the products you bring into your home, and you can put a houseplant in every nook of your nest.

Plants are the lungs of the planet, and the ability of houseplants to improve the quality of indoor air is an accepted scientific fact. Basically, plants are living, breathing air purifiers.

All plants clean and condition the air we breathe, but some plants are better at removing harmful pollutants than others. Here's a list of some of the best plants for purifying the air you breathe, and they're all lovely to boot!

Aloe vera: The thick, succulent, spiky leaves absorb carbon dioxide at night and make for a great bedroom plant. The thick juice inside the leaves is also good for soothing that sunburn!

Areca palm: A beautiful, graceful palm that's rated as one of the best houseplants for removing indoor air toxins.

Bamboo palm: Can you say gorgeous? The bamboo palm's long, slender canes and rich fans add an exotic flair to any room.

Dragon tree: This striking plant has a strong cane and long, narrow leaves edged with red. It adds great texture, color, and shape to any room.

Gerbera daisy: Who would have thought these big, bold, colorful daisies are so effective at removing toxins from the air?

Lady palm: One of the most popular and easiest houseplants to care for, its thick, shiny leaves are resistant to insects and excellent for removing toxins.

Moth orchid: Easier to grow than most orchids, the moth orchid's thick, leathery leaves, tall stem, and exotic blooms make it a beautiful addition to any nest.

Peace lily: Its lovely white spathes reveal a pointy flower that blooms indoors. The beautiful shape and serene color are very Zen.

Peacock plant: This plant get its name from the distinctive markings on its round, feathery, silvery and dark green leaves. Adds a strong dash of texture and color to any room.

Rubber plant: Its sleek, rounded, hearty leaves tolerate dim light and cooler temperatures—very easy to grow indoors, and very good for the air.

Flowers, girl!

If your back aches from endless hours hunched over a bag of potting soil, or if you've been talking your plants up so much you're canceling appointments with your therapist and yet your plants are still dying—it may be time to think about putting the watering can down. Just as with children and animals, some people have a knack for growing plants and some don't. A wilted Boston fern doesn't mean you love your plants any less than your neighbor with the indoor garden that could feed the whole block. Personally, I know plenty of plant-adept people who can't get anything to grow in their apartments except mold and mildew, so besides the you-factor, there are also the circumstances of your nest to take into consideration. The air may be too dry (try putting a plant in the bathroom or buy a humidifier), the radiator heat may be too intense—any number of factors may be keeping your plants from prospering. But the point I'm trying to make here is to stop beating yourself over the head for being a bad plant mommy. Plants die; it happens. And when it does, remember that you don't need to actually grow a plant to bring the luscious texture, color, and ambience of nature into your nest—just give flower arranging a spin! It's a fun and inexpensive way to freshen up your nest.

Many folks are intimidated by the thought of putting together a flower arrangement. Why? They're afraid of failing, of doing it wrong. They think that because it's an artistic endeavor, there must be a set of rules, a bag of inside tricks, a school one goes to in order to learn how to do it properly. Some of these assumptions are true, there are tricks and even schools, but there is only one rule: It doesn't matter if you know the difference between a peony and a petunia, a daffodil and a rhododendron, or bamboo and beach grass—all that matters is that you know what you like. Flower arranging is an art form where you make your own rules, follow your own instincts, and throw together colors, textures, and shapes that ultimately express how you feel. For example, if your man forgot your birthday, throw together a healthy bunch of reds and yellows and work out your powerful emotions. However, if he throws you the surprise birthday party of the year, place single stemmed roses all around your nest and keep the romantic memory lingering.

No matter what you feel like throwing together, remember that arranging should never be difficult. Quite the contrary, it should be effortless. The less effort you put into your arrangement the better, because the loveliest combinations are always those that look natural, uncontrived, and perfect in their imperfections. Sure, the flower shop on the corner probably has some ingeniously contrived arrangements, but don't even think about that. The true passion behind flower arranging, its true purpose, is also the true purpose of all nature: to inspire and make you feel good. So let's get at it.

Color happy

Step foot in any flower shop and you'll instantly be overwhelmed by all the shapes, textures, fragrances, and most of all, colors. As we explored in chapter two, Color Your Nest (pp. 9–22), color is a powerful thing, whether we're talking about paint or flowers. Red connotes strength and power, pink is all about softness and romance, orange emanates warmth and creativity, yellow is light and cheery, white is pure, and blue is calming and meditative. And, of course, you can't have a flower without a spat of green, the most natural and relaxing color of them all.

So what colors do you want in your arrangement? First of all, think about what the arrangement will be used for. If you're throwing a cocktail party, get it bubbling with a colorful array of red tulips, yellow daisies, and bright violets. If you're looking to embellish a romantic dinner table, maybe you want a single white orchid adorned with beach grass. Also think about the colors you already have in your nest. You can find a flower to bring out the green in your sofa, the violet in your drapes, the saffron of your walls, and even the blue in your eyes! Whatever colors you choose, they'll bring life to any room and help set a mood—but don't stress about it too much. Unlike choosing paint color for your walls, fresh-cut flowers usually last about five days, so there's no big commitment. Just go to the flower shop, survey the lot, and pick the colors your eye is naturally drawn to. Spot a luscious shade of red that makes you all warm inside? Grab it. See a lovely pink petal that makes your mouth water? Take that one, too. White is nice in any arrangement, maybe pick up a few of those and—see how much fun it can be? Just let it all go and dive in; but in case you're more frustrated than elated at all the color choices before you, here are three main color schemes to give your picking more purpose.

The all-one-color arrangement: Same-color arrangements are simple yet powerful. Use them if you really want to make a color statement (see the color horoscopes on page 12.) Imagine an all-red arrangement in a stark-white room; all blue against an orange wall; or a slathering of buttery yellow in a room flooded with natural light.

The family arrangement: Using different shades within the same color family is a more subtle and harmonious approach to color. Imagine an arrangement of pastel yellows, warm yellows, and autumn golds; or stark whites, linen whites, and rich creams. Delicious!

The mix-it-up arrangement: A multicolored arrangement is all about contrasts, bursts, and complements. Get as wild and crazy as you want, but using complementary colors (page 15) will keep the combinations looking pro.

The flower shop

Unless you're lucky enough to have your own garden, your flower arranging adventure will begin at your local flower shop. If you don't already have a favorite, choose one that has plenty of people buzzing around it. A busy flower shop is not only a sign that people are happy with the flowers, it also means the inventory goes out the door quickly, so the flowers are likely to be fresh.

The shop's buckets upon buckets of colorful, fragrant flowers are sure to be intoxicating, but do try to keep your wits about you. Choose flowers with petals that feel crisp, not limp, between your fingers; make sure the heads and stems are free of bruises. Stems should be firm and healthy green, never dark or slimy. You should also take the stage of the bloom into consideration. If the flower is tightly closed, it may never bloom, whereas if it's already fully open, it's past its peak. Basically, you want to pick a basketful of young, virile, healthy flowers that will peak after you get them home.

Growing your own

If you're lucky enough to have a flower patch of your own, cut the flowers in the early part of the day, before the sun zaps them. Carry a bucket around with you and plunge the fresh-cut stems into clean water as soon as they're cut. Choose flowers that aren't quite in full bloom, and leave the younger buds behind to mature and be picked another sunny morning.

Taking them home

Don't even think about leaving the flower shop with a fresh, hand-picked bunch only to take them on a hot car or subway ride home and then forget about them. Fresh-cut flowers are fragile creatures. They've literally been cut off from their natural sources of nutrients and water, and while they don't need a whole lot of care, they do need it in a timely manner.

As soon as you get your flowers home, take off any strangling plastic wrapping, rubber bands, or ties from the flower shop. With a knife or scissors, cut the ends of the stems at a sharp diagonal. This allows the stems to rest on a point when they're in their vase or other container, making it easier for them to suck up water. Next, pull or cut off any bruised petals, sharp thorns, and leaves that may end up falling below the waterline (submerged leaves will rot and contaminate the water.) Then put the whole bunch in a clean bucket of water and let it sit overnight in a cool, dark place. The stems will be sealing off their pores soon, and you want to give them one last, long drink. Filling the bucket with tepid water instead of cold will allow more oxygen to travel through the stems, and adding a little flower food to the water will give the petals a surefire lift. You can buy food at the flower shop or make your own with the recipe below.

Flower food: Mix 1/2 capful of bleach and 2 teaspoons of sugar to every 1 gallon of tepid water. This sugary concoction nourishes your flowers, encourages baby buds to develop, and helps keep bacteria away.

Flower revival

If you get home at 2:00 in the morning only to find the flowers you left on the counter earlier have wilted, there's still hope. Before you go to bed, set the stems in a bucket or sink of tepid water, add a little flower food, and let them sit overnight in a cool, dark place. The next morning, refill the bucket with tepid water, and completely submerge the flowers for one hour (see page 113). It's sure to give droopy petals a lift!

Shaping it up

Flowers, like people, come in all shapes and sizes. There are meaty birds of paradise and phallic lilies; thin, willowy wildflowers and soft cones of lilacs; sunflowers that grow to be six feet tall and delicate violets you can hold in the palm of your hand. With such an amazing array of shapes and sizes, your arrangement can be short or tall, round or angular, bountiful or sparse, and anything in between. You might think the shape and size of your arrangement is mostly dependent on the types of flowers you use—but that's not entirely true. By utilizing a few tricks of the trade, you'll find you can shape your arrangement almost any way you fancy.

The right container

Whether it's a tall glass vase, an antique pitcher, a Vegas shot glass, or a hollowed-out piece of bamboo, the container you put your flowers in will impact the way your arrangement looks. A tall, thin container will keep your flowers straight and at attention, whereas a lower, rounder container is a good home if you want a soft, rounder arrangement. Containers with large openings are good for bountiful arrangements, or if you just have a few flowers you can place them over and across one another for a minimalist yet dynamic presentation. Containers with small openings are only good for displaying a few flowers, otherwise they get packed in like a rush-hour subway.

When it comes to choosing a container, think outside the traditional glass vase. Almost anything that holds water can be used as a vase; even if it doesn't hold water, just put the flowers in a smaller vase and tuck it inside where nobody will see! From an old soda or wine bottle (buy a bottle cutter at any craft store and cut the top off), to small wooden tea boxes, to imported coffee cans, to terra cotta planters, to a fishbowl (minus the fish), to an old cowboy boot, hunting down the perfect container is part of the fun.

Tip: Try to select a container before you start cutting and arranging your stems. Then as you're building your bouquet, you can put them in their new home every so often and see how they're really going to look.

The right cut

One of the easiest ways to shape your arrangement is to play with the length of your stems. Obviously, a flower with a long stem is going to be tall, and it's probably going to bend over and look rounded and soft. On the flip side, a shorter stem is going to stand up straight and look more rigid. Cutting all of the stems the same length will create a clean, structured shape; varying the lengths will give the arrangement a more natural, unexpected flair.

Making arrangements

Once you've soaked and snipped, container hunted and cut, it's finally time to bring it all together. Creating a fabulous arrangement should never be difficult, but that doesn't mean you want to just grab a handful of stems and shove them into an old wine bottle filled with water. Think of creating your arrangement as putting together a drop-dead party outfit—you want it to inspire, flatter, and turn heads.

First, put on music to put you in a creative mood. Then take a few flowers out of the bunch and either hold them in your hand or lay them out on a flat surface. These flowers should be the ones you want for the centerpiece of your arrangement, your starting point. Now add and subtract flowers around this initial centerpiece, playing with different shapes and color and texture combinations until you find a look that's just right. Experiment, mix it up, and start all over again. This is not the place for perfectionism, you want to just have fun with it. Trying to make it look like something out of *Better Homes and Gardens* will only leave you with an arrangement that looks contrived and forced, not relaxed, natural, and personal.

Magic tricks

Throwing a big party? Boyfriend's mom coming to dinner? Want to create an arrangement that looks more like art? It's time to whip out the bag of tricks, especially the florist's wire and tape (get them at flower shops and hardware stores), and any kind of ties. You can twist, turn, and wrap flowers around each other and other objects until you find a presentation Picasso would be proud of; then wire,

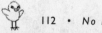

tape, or tie everything into place. Here are a few inside tips to help you shape, straighten, submerge, and create an awe-inspiring, jaw-dropping, even gravity-defying arrangement.

Lift and separate: Like your arrangement but the flowers still aren't falling into place how you pictured it? Defy gravity. Twist and turn the stems around each other until you find a perfectly perky, robust, or contoured shape, then hold it all together by wrapping wire or florist's tape around it. Take it easy on the wire and tape though. Tuck it in and tie it off with a clean finish so it doesn't steal the show!

Straightening stems: Some flowers, like tulips and gerberas, naturally have crooked stems. Sometimes this can look fabulously raw, but if you prefer the polished look of a straight stem, here's what you can do. Take some florist's wire and insert it at the base of the flower head. Then take the remainder of the wire and twist it around and down the stem. The wire acts as a brace and will help it straighten out.

Wrap it up: Wrapping your bouquet in a lush palm or banana leaf, handmade paper, or even a piece of sheer fabric is a beautiful way to add color, texture, and interest. Form the bouquet in your hand, and being careful not to wrap the flowers too tightly together, secure them with a rubber band. Now take your wrap and lay it out on a flat surface. Place the bouquet in the middle, and fold the wrap over the stems, just as you'd fold a baby up in a blanket, and make sure the stems stick out of the bottom so they can still drink water once in the container. Now tie the wrap up nicely with twine, hemp, ribbon, or wire.

Floating and drowning: A bowl full of floating flowers is a quick yet gorgeous arrangement for that last-minute party or special guest. Just snip your flowers' stems down to an inch or so and float them in a big bowl full of water, the wider the mouth the better. Go crazy with different colors, textures, and sizes of flowers; change the water every day, and it should stay fresh for a few days. A completely submerged flower won't last quite as long, but the effect is fabulously tranquil. Just find yourself a pretty rock (bleached ones are available at flower shops), or something that's heavy but clean. Wrap a piece of florist's wire around and under the rock, secure with a twist, and then wind the wire around the bottom of a flower's stem.

Leave a bit of wire between the rock and the stem, place the two in a glass container, and fill with water until the flower is completely submerged, anchored by the rock, and seemingly floats underwater.

Marbles, rocks, and berries: Colored marbles and ornamental stones are sold by the bagful at flower shops and home stores for the sole purpose of adding color, texture, and interest to your clear flower containers. You can also find them on the cheap at pet supply stores for use in aquariums, but why pay for them at all? Rummage around your apartment for colorful items such as beads, sea glass, and broken terra cotta pieces; let them soak in a little bleach diluted with water, rinse, then throw them on in. Even colorful cranberries, lemons, unripe whole coffee beans, kumquats, and other hard-skinned fruits and berries can add a fabulous splash of color to the right container and its arrangement.

Flower frogs: Flower frogs are made of everything from stone to wire to colored glass, and they sit at the bottom of the container and hold your arrangement in place. How? They have little compartments, slots, or wires that hold stems in place. They're sold at flower shops and garden stores, and can help keep your arrangement perfectly relaxed and carefree, or as perfectly stiff as a prom hairdo. If you want the structure but don't want to spend the money, taping a grid across the mouth of your container (like a tic-tac-toe) and then placing the stems in the slots will also help keep the stems in place.

Flower power

Everybody knows that red roses symbolize love, but what about daisies, lilies, orchids, or even white roses? Here's a list of what some flowers traditionally symbolize, just in case you want to pick your flowers with a purpose.

* Red carnation: I'm sorry
* White chrysanthemum: Truth
* Daffodil: Warm regards
* Daisy: Innocence

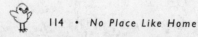

* Gardenia: Secret admirer!
* Jasmine: Friendship
* White lilacs: Youth
* Purple lilacs: First love
* Narcissus: Stay sweet
* Orchid: Fertility
* Pink rose: Perfect happiness
* Sunflower: Pride
* Thornless rose: Love at first sight
* White rose: Purity
* Tulip: Luck
* Violet: Faith
* Viscera: Let's dance!

DIY wrist corsage

Fresh corsages aren't just for proms anymore, and they're so easy to make! Just take a single flower and cut the stem so it's very short. Wrap thin florist's wire around the stem, and then entwine it with a favorite bracelet. You can attach a single fragrant bloom, or several smaller blooms; it's up to you. Try color coordinating your bracelet and the blooms, maybe a pink rose in full bloom on a pink pearl necklace, or a yellow orchid on a bracelet with green semiprecious stones, how lovely! Once the flower and bracelet are wired together, go over the ends of the wire with florist's tape so you don't scratch up your skin. Wear your creation to a special party or just out on a beautiful spring day—you're sure to turn heads!

PART THREE

· ·

Flock It!

My life changed drastically when I moved to New York City. I went from a spacious West Coast house with apple trees in the backyard to a tiny Manhattan apartment where the trees grew through holes in the sidewalks. But I loved it. The theaters, restaurants, and people were amazing; and small as it may have been, I loved my apartment because it was right smack in the middle of it all. I may not have had a huge kitchen to cook in, but I could always order takeout. I may not have had a lot of space, but I consolidated my belongings and went out a lot. I adapted nicely to my new NYC lifestyle, but after awhile I began to feel that something was missing—my friends. It wasn't that I didn't have a handful of wonderful new friends, mind you, it was just that I never had any of them over because my apartment was so tiny, and everybody always went out anyway. What I missed was the more nesty side of socializing, the staying-in part. I decided to hostess a book club at my place, and the Crumpet Club eventually bloomed into a once-a-month happy hour where my friends and I would get together and share good food, okay wine, and great conversation. Of course, the idea was to discuss the noted book of the month, but the conversation always seemed to sway toward job and relationship problems, my new furnishing additions, and who's cuter, Jude Law or Viggo Mortensen. It was all great fun, but the best part was that all the love, laughter, and good energy lingered on in my nest, long after everyone had gone home.

Bring It On Home

· ·

Going out with your friends is always a good time. You slip into your foxiest threads, layer on the lip gloss, set the do, and head out to set the evening ablaze. But more times than not, you end up standing in a crowded bar, yelling at your friends over blaring music, and paying $10 for a less-than-marvelous martini. Yes, it's all fun, but sometimes you feel the need for some quality time with your friends, listening to your own music, sharing good stories, drinking too much red wine, and getting as silly or serious as you want, all in the privacy of your own home. Lucky for you, you've got what it takes to make these wonderful times happen—a fabulous nest.

You've surely developed a loving relationship with your home space by now. You've known it since it was an empty space with white walls and bare cupboards; and you've nurtured it into your very own, very special space. What a glorious feeling to have such a space, and what an even more glorious feeling to share this love.

Whether it's a well-organized get-together like a monthly book club or just an impulse girls' night in—it's time to bring the house down by staying in for a change. Have the gang over for a wine-tasting party, a group spa day, or a Stitch 'n Bitch, and share your space while celebrating the sanctity of friendship. There's nothing quite like the intimacy of a private party in your own home, so get on the horn and get your friends together. Share your space. Spread the love.

Things That Make You Go Mmm . . .

W ant to have the girls over but you're too pooped to pull a full-fledged party theme out of a hat? Nothing gets the gang over faster than a night of good food, drinks, and conversation. A food- or drink-focused event is perfect when you're in a time pinch or want to hang with a smaller, tighter crowd. You could put on the apron and throw a fabulous, five-course Thai dinner party—but first of all, I thought you were pooped, and second of all, why bother? Just lay out the food and cork the wine (winespeak for remove the cork) or put the teakettle on, and they will come. Here are some fun and simple food- and drink-centric ideas that are sure to keep the mouths watering, the laughter flowing, and the lips flapping well into the wee hours.

Wine-oh!

Wine brings people together, so get the girls over for a night of wine tasting! It doesn't have to be expensive. You can pick up plenty a great bottle of wine for $15, and several good ones around the $10 mark, too. Have at least one bottle on hand for when your guests arrive, and ask each of your friends to bring over a bottle, too. Instant theme: BYOW! You can even cap the price if you wish. Just make sure you set a rule for the party: the wine should either be red or white and never both—unless you have ibuprofen as party favors and nothing planned until 2:00 the next day.

So how do you go about picking out a decent bottle to get the party started? Just remember, throwing a wine-tasting party is about having fun and discovering what you and your friends like, so don't be intimidated by the bottles upon bottles at the wine store, the books upon books at the bookstore, or even your wine-finicky friends. Wine is always semi-subjective. What's rich and full-bodied to some may be too sweet or oaky for others.

If you really know nothing about wine, the best thing to do is let someone else choose for you. Go into a wine store, tell them the type of wine you're looking for—for example, Cabernet, Merlot, Chardonnay, etc.—and how much you want to spend. Chances are they'll be able to fix you up with a few bottles to fit your description. If the wine store is especially fancy, they may even have a sommelier (wine specialist) on staff, and if that's the case, they can not only suggest what wine to buy, they can also suggest the best foods to accompany it. It's like having your very own personal party planner!

Red, red wine

Red wines vary in taste more than white wines, and because of this, many people will swear up and down that red is the only "true" wine. Red wines have more tannin, a substance found in the skins of the grapes that can best be described as that bitter dryness that gives red its backbone. Reds are usually characterized as being one of the following: light-bodied with low tannin; medium-bodied with moderate tannin; or full-bodied and tannic (highest in tannin). But keep in mind that red wines don't always fit so easily into one of these categories, as you'll see below.

Red is meant to be served at room temperature and is usually what people drink with a meal. Unless, of course, you're sitting inside on a cold, rainy night, then it *is* the meal. Here are some of the better-known reds:

Cabernet Sauvignon: A medium-to-full-bodied, high-tannin wine often described as tasting of black currants.

Merlot: A full-bodied, low-tannin wine that can hint of chocolate.

Pinot Noir: A full-bodied, medium-to-low-tannin wine that may be either fruity or earthy.

Syrah/Shiraz: A full-bodied, high-tannin wine that can taste of berries, smoke, spice, or even burned rubber.

Classic white

Unlike red, white wines are usually considered aperitif wines, meaning wines that are consumed before dinner, but plenty of people drink them with dinner, after dinner, and again, even *as* dinner. When served with food, however, white usually goes better with lighter fare. Most whites are either dry and crisp, or dry and full-bodied with an oaky character. Whites are meant to be served chilled, but not so cold that they lose their flavor. Needless to say, on a hot summer day, a white-wine tasting party is definitely in order. Here are some of the more popular whites:

Chardonnay: A crisp, oaky, full-bodied, dry wine. In short, a good glass of Chardonnay has it all going on! It can hint of toast, smoke, vanilla, or even earth, but watch out: cheap bottles can be sickeningly sweet.

Pinot Gris: A not-so-crisp (otherwise known as flabby), medium-to-full-bodied wine that may carry a fruity aroma.

Riesling: A crisp, light-bodied and refreshing wine that's traditionally known as being sweet, fruity, and flowery, but isn't always that way.

Sauvignon Blanc: A definitively crisp, light-to-medium-bodied, dry wine that may hint of herbs, grass, or fruit.

Think pink

Rosé wine is a refreshing summer alternative for the red wine drinker. While it's made from red grapes, it usually lacks the color and tannin of red wines, and the oakiness of white. European rosés are usually dry, while Americans are sweet. Rosé should be served cool, but not as cold as you would serve white wine.

Winespeak

A wine-tasting party is almost as much about talking as it is about tasting. After all, sharing your wine experience with a group is just like sharing your reading experience with a book club. You want to talk about it, discuss it, and communicate as clearly as possible. But in order to do this most effectively, first you (and your guests) must learn some of the lingo—or winespeak. Here are some key words to put you in the know.

* Sweet: A fruity, berrylike, sugary, jammy, or even sticky taste.
* Dry: Not sweet.
* Crisp: If it has a bite, it's acidic, and if it's acidic, it's crisp. Usually used to describe white wines; crispness gives white wine its backbone.
* Flabby: A wine with no backbone. It's low in acidity and not crisp.
* Tannin: A sometimes bitter dryness detected in the back of your throat; the backbone of red wine.
* Aroma: The smell; a complex aroma is sometimes called a "bouquet."
* Body: The weight and size of the wine in your mouth; some wines really do feel bigger than others!
* Depth: The layers of taste—a fine wine is never flat.
* Complexity: When a wine keeps revealing new layers of flavor, or depths, it's considered complex.
* Balance: The relationship of all the different characteristics to one another. A wine is balanced if one characteristic, say sweetness or dryness, doesn't stand out.
* Finish: The impression a wine leaves in your mouth after you've swallowed it. The encore!

Swirl it, smell it, taste it

So how do you make sure your soiree is a true-to-life wine-tasting party and not just a party where everybody drinks wine? Do your best to shift the focus from gossip and job talk to wine talk, while also slowing down the drinking process. Take measures to ensure that the group discovers and discusses how certain wines look, smell, and taste; and pair different wines with different foods to see how the taste buds react. In short, you want your guests to sip the wine, savor the food, and discuss the bottle of the moment, not the man of the moment. In any case, this amount of discipline may call for a personal demonstration of proper tasting etiquette.

If you've ever been to a wine-tasting event, you probably know that the tasting process is really made up of three separate steps: swirling, smelling, and tasting. Start off by pouring a small amount of wine into your glass and looking at it. Hold it in front of a white background (a white wall or tablecloth will do) and carefully observe the color. Red wines aren't just red; they can range from a pale red to deep brown red, and they usually become lighter as they age. Did you know that white wines aren't really white? They range from green to yellow to brown. A richly colored white wine usually means more flavor and age; if it's really brown, it may mean that the bottle's gone bad, so sip carefully. While time improves a red wine, it ruins most whites.

Place your glass down on a flat surface, and rotate it so that the wine swirls around and coats the inside of the glass. Notice the "legs" of the wine—these are the liquid shapes it makes as it runs down the side. Good, thick legs may indicate a thicker body and a higher alcohol content and/or sweetness level. Now bring the glass up to your nose, close your eyes, and take a long, deep whiff. Call out whatever comes to mind: wood, earth, plums, grass, coffee, chocolate, a double tall vanilla Frappuccino. Discover and explore the subtle nuances of the aromas. Hopefully they're all good smells, but if you do get a wine that smells of vinegar, leather, or an old shoe, take note of that as well. Part of the wine-tasting process is learning what you don't like as much as learning what you do like. If your nose gets tired, keep a bowl of roasted coffee beans or a piece of bread nearby to sniff and clear the nasal palate.

After sniffing the wine, it's finally time to taste. Take a medium-sized sip, hold it in your mouth, and draw some air in through your mouth and over your tongue. You want to add air to the wine because many of wine's more subtle tastes are actually aromas. Now swish the wine around in your mouth—like you're chewing it—not like mouthwash, and swallow. Notice how it finishes off. Does the taste linger? Change? Turn bitter?

Cheers!

You now know what to do with a corked bottle, and how to talk about it like a pro...so get the party started! Call the friends, cube the cheeses, and put out the oyster crackers; but instead of just lining the bottles and glasses on the table, why not throw a few unexpected twists into the evening and turn it into a four-star event?

Merlot challenge: Have everybody bring a specific type of wine, say Merlot; but have some people bring cheap bottles, while others can share the cost of more expensive ones. Then put a piece of paper over the labels so that nobody knows which bottle is which, sniff, swirl, taste, and judge. Try to rate them in terms of price. You just might be surprised!

Piggyback party: Find out what your wines' characteristics are—if a bottle is chocolaty, fruity, berrylike, nutty, etc. (you can call up the wine store and ask if you need to). Then place a small bowl of chocolate, fruit, berries, and so on by the bottle so that after your guests take a sip, they can piggyback a taste of the complementary food and enhance the wine's flavor!

Wine and food mixer: Lay out a super spread of cheeses, fruits, breads, chocolates, and any other goodies you fancy. Then have each guest take a sip of wine and see how their reactions change when they follow the same wine with different foods. They may discover that tannic reds make food seem less sweet (a very tannic red balances out a super-sweet dessert); crisp, acidic whites are good with sweets and cheeses; and a sweet wine can either emphasize a sweet dish or balance out a salty one. Do be careful if your wine selection mixes the reds and whites—the combination is fabulous for food-tasting purposes but can give you quite the headache if you don't watch it.

Killer combo party: No fancy tricks here, just a killer combination of wines and food. Some tantalizing hors d'oeuvres that always go well with wine are: dark and semisweet chocolate, toasted almonds and walnuts, green olives, smoked oysters and smoked salmon, Gorgonzola cheese, goat cheese, blue cheese, and actually, just about any kind of cheese. And don't forget the bread and oyster crackers to cleanse the palate.

Organic wine party: Does sulfite-free, organic wine taste better than traditionally treated wine? That's subjective, but many organic winemakers claim that healthy, organic grapes make for better wine. Get a few bottles of organic and enjoy a sulfite-free night, maybe even partner it up with organic fruits, veggies, and cheese! (See below for more about organic wines.)

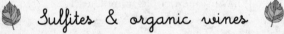

Sulfites & organic wines

If you look at any wine label, chances are it says "Contains Sulfites." Sulfur dioxide is a compound that's added to most wines to keep it from going bad. While sulfur has been used in the winemaking process since Roman times, there's a lot of hype surrounding it lately because many people are finding out they're sensitive to it. If you're sulfite-sensitive, you should know that dry red wine has the least amount, followed by dry white. Sweet wines contain the most sulfites to keep all that sugar from fermenting. If you want to go sulfite-free, try choosing from the ever-expanding organic wine aisle, but do be careful when reading labels. "Made from organically grown grapes" means the grapes are organic, but sulfites may have been added. The label "Organic wine" is the real deal—no chemicals in the soil, no chemicals on the grapes, no chemicals in the wine. Better for the earth, better for you—but a better-tasting wine? That's your call; but many winemakers are doing organic not for the extra marketing push but because they do believe a better grape makes a better wine.

Wine is such an involved, complex, and subjective subject, it's easy to become overwhelmed—and even intimidated. If all of this information is a bit daunting, just give wine-tasting a test run before you throw your own party. Plenty of wine and liquor stores hold casual wine-tasting events, and they're usually free. Spend an afternoon sampling wine as you learn about it! You're sure to have a good time—how can you not with all those people standing around just waiting to refill your glass?

Taking tea

Tea is hot, and not just in temperature. In a day and age when you can hardly walk a city block without bumping into a Starbucks, tea is quickly gaining in popularity and bringing a fresh, healthy perspective to a country famous for its constant grande double latte buzz.

Like a fine wine, tea offers an exquisitely palatable array of tastes and aromas, and nuances of body and character. You can enjoy a steamy cup of grassy sencha, floral jasmine, toasty English breakfast, or piney Earl Grey. You can sip on black tea, green tea, blended tea, iced tea, or spiced tea. You can take milk, honey, lemon, or sugar. But no matter how you choose to sip it, each cup offers a quiet, meditative moment, a quick afternoon pick-me-up, a cold day warm-you-up, and a great reason to get together with your tea-lovin' friends.

World tea party

Legend has it that tea was first discovered by a Chinese emperor when some leaves from a tea tree accidentally blew into his pot of boiling water. From that point on, tea has held a strong influence in religious, social, and spiritual ceremonies around the world. In Japan, the serving of tea has been elevated to an art form with the Japanese tea ceremony, called the chanoyu. In Russia, tea was taken with a slice of lemon, and either a spoonful of raspberry jam or a sugar cube held between the teeth. In Morocco, shopkeepers greet prospective customers with a glass of sweet mint tea; Tibetans drink home-churned, salty butter tea all day—and it's considered rude to refuse a cup, even if the salty taste makes you wince.

Types of tea

All black and green tea comes from the same tree, an evergreen shrub that grows in countries like China, India, Japan, and Sri Lanka. And just like wine, the climate and soil conditions all contribute to the subtle characteristics of any batch of leaves. But what really sets one category of tea apart from another is how the leaves are processed. Black tea is the most processed and contains the most caffeine; green tea is the least processed and contains the least caffeine and the most healthy antioxidants; and Oolong tea is a mix between black and green teas, in taste and caffeine content.

Tea blends

Tea companies create their own special blends, and market niches, by mixing several types of leaves into one package. Here are some of the more popular blends—taste varies from brand to brand.

Black

Assam: Grown in the northeastern Indian state of Assam, this black tea is a staple and can be enjoyed anywhere, anytime. Dress it up with milk and honey, or take it plain.

Ceylon: With a hearty yet delicately flavored brew, Ceylon teas are especially good in the morning with milk.

Darjeeling: Darjeeling is a light and lovely tea grown high in the Himalayas. Its brew has a bright golden color and delicate, flowery aroma.

Keemun: A Chinese tea with a rich red brew and smoky aroma. Its full body makes it a true tea lover's tea.

Lapsang Souchong: This pungent tea is smoked over pine wood for a unique, smoky flavor. Delicious with milk and honey.

Green

Dragonwell: An emerald-green tea with a very "green tasting" liquor. A good choice for hard-core green-tea lovers.

Genmaicha: A hearty tea blended with toasted rice kernels; it has a dry, nutty flavor.

Gunpowder/pearl tea: Young tips and buds are rolled into small pellets for a slightly grassy brew that's perfect for afternoon.

Sencha: The classic Japanese tea. Its bright green brew and freshly-cut-grass liquor is too green for some, but others love it.

Flavored, scented & special blends

Earl Grey: Bergamot essential oil is what gives this tea its sharp, crisp aroma. The unique taste is best served straight up, hold the milk, hold the sugar.

English breakfast: A strong, full-bodied breakfast favorite, usually made from a blend of Indian and Ceylon teas. Tasty with milk and sugar.

Irish breakfast: An even heartier tea than English breakfast, this one definitely calls for mellowing out with milk and sugar.

Jasmine: Made by scenting green tea with fresh jasmine buds, this blend is fragrant, floral, and fabulous.

Russian blend: A strong black tea with a smoky aroma, usually from the addition of Lapsang Souchong leaves.

Bag it or loose it?

For many tea lovers, that is the question. Bagged tea is premeasured and easy to tuck in the purse and take to work. However, many people prefer to brew tea the slower, old-fashioned way—with loose leaves and a tea ball (infuser) or strainer. If you use a tea ball, don't pack it too full as this will inhibit the leaves from opening and releasing their flavor (if you like strong tea, just use two half-full tea balls instead of one). When using a strainer, simply fill it with tea, place it over your teapot or cup, and pour hot water up above the tea line.

Top five brewing tips

There are many ways to brew tea, from the Japanese ceremony in which powdered tea is whisked into a frothy liquid, to the Tibetan tradition of churning tea, butter, and salt with a wooden piston. In the west, most tea drinkers prepare tea the Chinese way—by boiling water and adding leaves. Simple as the preparation is, there are five steps you can take to help ensure you brew a tasty cup every time.

1. Make sure your kettle is clean. A dirty, soapy, or residue-ridden kettle will alter and even ruin the delicate taste of your tea. Wash and dry your kettle every couple of weeks, and give the interior a good scrub with a brush and some baking soda once a month to help prevent mineral deposits from building up.

2. Use good, clean water. If the water from your tap tastes bad, your tea will taste bad. For the best taste, use filtered water or even bottled water. If the kettle's been sitting on the stove since morning, refresh the water before brewing your afternoon cup.

3. Use the right amount of water at the right temperature. Some teas require fewer leaves than others for a full-bodied cup; experiment to find the perfect combination. Green tea should never be steeped in boiling water; let water sit for five minutes before pouring it over your green leaves. Oolong tea should be steeped with steamy but not boiling water; steep hearty black teas in boiling water.

4. Brew for a spell. Don't just dunk the tea bag until the water turns brown, as the color of the brew isn't necessarily reflective of how strong it will taste. Tea leaves need to open and release their flavor. Green teas usually need to be steeped for 1 to 3 minutes, Oolong and black teas for 3 to 5 minutes.

5. Serve fresh. Tea is always best when fresh and hot—always brew a fresh cup rather than throwing a cold cup in the microwave. If tea does get cold, make ice cubes out of it and use in iced tea!

Tip: Store your tea in an airtight container and keep in a cool, dark place. The leaves may look lovely displayed in a clear glass jar, but light will only zap them of their freshness. If you use tea bags, store them in an airtight container, too. It's best to use any tea within six months to a year.

Serving the perfect cup

You could boil water in an old pan and drink your tea out of old coffee mugs, but as serving tea is considered an art form in many places around the globe, why not take advantage of the astounding array of kettles, teapots, and teacups available? Some of the designs are downright righteous, and they're good conversation pieces at your tea party to boot!

You can pick and choose a teapot to fit any decor, mood, or cere-mony. Japanese cast-iron kettles, called tetsubins, are wonderful to

 Teaspeak

Just as with wine tasting, tea tasting is an art form with its own lingo. Here are some of the more common terms used to describe the different nuances of tea:

* Aroma: The smell; a complex aroma is sometimes called a "bouquet."
* Astringency: A puckery sensation comparable to tannins in red wines.
* Body: The sensation of weight and substance: it's either thin, medium, or full.
* Full: The tea's liquor has strength and is well-rounded.
* Liquor: The liquid; the brew.
* Thick: Describes a liquor that has substance, minus the strength.
* Thin: Lacking in thickness and strength; watery.
* Toasty: A smoky taste.

look at and because the interiors are unglazed, the iron becomes seasoned over time, much like an iron skillet. Chinese yixing teapots are also unglazed and come in wonderfully inventive shapes and sizes, but are very small and intended to brew one only cup at a time. Carved Chinese jade teapots are thought to bring good luck to the user, and beautiful English teapots, usually made of china, come in lovely shapes and with hand-painted designs. Matching cups (Western-style with handles, Eastern-style without) are usually available, and might be worth the investment. Go to www.holymtn.com or www.harney.com to get an idea of all the tea accessories to drool over.

Milk, sugar, or lemon?

Oolong and green teas have such a delicate palate, they're usually best plain. The exception is to add a few drops of honey, which can be nice. Black teas are delicious served with milk, honey, sugar, or lemon; or in Russian tea, a traditional dollop of raspberry jam! Whatever you fancy in your tea, never use cream. While milk has a protein called casein that actually binds with tea to enhance its flavor, cream has less of this protein and its effect is much different—it actually drowns out the taste of the tea.

DIY tea party

So, what tea traditions are you fixing to practice at your party? Are you going to do it proper like the English and serve high tea with crumpets and finger sandwiches at exactly 6:00 in the evening, or are you going to hold an elaborate ceremony that celebrates an enlightened life? Are you going to drink homemade iced tea with a sprig of fresh mint on a hot summer's day, or just lounge around and drink Lipton while watching old Elvis movies? How you choose to take your tea isn't important. At the heart of every tea party, from Liverpool to your living room, is to get together with friends and share a cup. But if you do want to go with a tea-party theme, here are a few good ones to get you started.

Afternoon tea: Get out your best china, lacy linens, and white gloves, and have the girls over for a proper English afternoon tea.

Originally invented as a tide-me-over between an early breakfast and a late dinner, afternoon tea was a social obsession in England during the Victorian era, and it's still widely practiced today. Send out proper invites, and make sure teatime falls between the traditional three and four o'clock in the afternoon. Plan to serve your guests light fare such as finger sandwiches, scones, pastries, and, of course, English tea. Make it a society event, full of classical music, pearls, and juicy gossip. To get everyone in the Victorian state of mind, watch the high-society antics of *House of Mirth* or *The Age of Innocence* on DVD as you daintily sip at your tea.

High tea: The same idea as afternoon tea, but this party takes place from six o'clock in the evening on, and with heartier hors d'oeuvres. At high tea, you'll want to offer your guests cheese, meats, breads, and cakes.

Japanese tea ceremony: The chanoyu is a beautiful but extremely detailed ritual (see below). To throw your own chanoyu, it might be best to create a relaxing, Japanese-inspired ambience and not go through the entire ceremony—it can last up to five hours! Put the word out by sending invitations made of rice paper, and ask guests to wear Asian-inspired clothing—even kimonos! Put on some traditional Japanese music; place pillows on the floor for everyone to sit on; get crafty and make origami place settings. When guests arrive, bow to them to show your respect, and have them remove their shoes at the door. Traditionally, green tea is served at a chanoyu, with light snacks such as sweets made of red bean paste. If you don't like bean paste, serve sushi or mochi ice cream, delicious little ice cream cakes you can buy at most Asian supermarkets.

Snacks

Teatime snacks should be light and fresh. Scones, shortbread, fresh pastries, and all cookies are a good choice, as are crumpets, warm biscuits, and cake. If you have the time, whip up some tiny tea sandwiches with avocado, cucumber, tomato, and basil; or if you're crunched for time, Nilla wafers and animal cookies are always a hit.

Tea and Zen

The Japanese tea ceremony, or chanoyu, was conceived by ancient Zen Buddhist priests as a meditation on purity, harmony, respect, and tranquility. In its most traditional form, the ceremony is an elaborately demonstrated practice of all four principles and can last four or five hours. A small, black lacquer container, a natsume, contains the matcha, the powdered Japanese green tea. It's carefully measured out with a bamboo spoon, a chashaku, and the matcha is then mixed with hot water and whisked until it makes a rich, frothy, sea-green liquid. The tea is then poured into a china bowl and served to the honorable guests. The guests turn the bowl three times and consume it in three sips. The bowl is then wiped three times with a silk cloth, refilled, and passed on to the next guest. There are many interpretations of why everything in this ceremony is done in threes—one is that the number 3 symbolizes good luck.

Drink to your health

In ancient China, tea was used to cure just about everything from headaches and depression to constipation. Today, medical journals throughout the world are reporting that tea reduces the risk of certain cancers and heart disease, lowers blood sugar levels, and prevents bad breath, viral infections, and even tooth decay. Most recently, everybody has been raving about the specific health benefits of green tea. Packed with antioxidants that help defend your body against free radicals, which cause everything from cancer and osteoporosis to premature aging of the skin and cardiovascular disease, green tea is also rich in B vitamins, riboflavin, niacin, folic acid, potassium, and magnesium; contains vitamin C in amounts comparable to lemon, and has more fluoride than fluoridated water!

Tea with a twist

For all you tea divas who want a fresh take on the traditional tea party—tea isn't always served piping hot and with your choice of milk, sugar, or lemon. It can be served iced or spiced, sun-soaked or even with a shot of tequila. Read on.

Iced tea

Iced tea was invented at the 1904 St. Louis World's Fair when a plantation owner was trying to give away hot samples on a hot day. Having no success, he threw a few ice cubes into the tea and his refreshing invention was the hit of the fair.

Get it:

4 cups cold water
¼ cup black tea leaves or
4 tea bags

Ice cubes
2 tablespoons sugar, to taste

Make it (hot-water method): Bring 2 cups cold water to boil in a saucepan. Remove from heat, add tea leaves or bags, cover, and steep for five minutes. If you're using loose-leaf tea, strain the mixture. Pour brew into a glass with the other 2 cups cold water. Stir, and add sugar or a squeeze of fresh lemon if you fancy. Serve poured over ice.

Make it (cold-water method): Pour all four cups of water into a pitcher and add tea leaves or bags. Stir, and let sit overnight in the refrigerator. If you're using loose-leaf tea, strain before you serve. Makes one frosty glass.

Thai iced tea

The Thai are known for their quintessential cooking, and their iced tea is no exception. This sweet, rich concoction packs a creamy kick with coconut and condensed milk.

Get it:

2 cups water
4 stars of anise, ground
1 tablespoon powdered vanilla
   or 1 teaspoon vanilla extract
Pinch of ground cloves

Pinch of ground cinnamon
3 cups black tea leaves
1 cup sweetened condensed milk
4 cups light coconut milk
crushed ice

Make it: Combine water, spices, and tea leaves in a saucepan and bring to a boil for five minutes, stirring constantly. Remove from heat, cover, and steep for one hour or until cool. Strain into a pitcher and stir in coconut milk. Put crushed ice in a glass, pour condensed milk over the top, and let it drip to the bottom. Add tea. Serve with a spoon. Serves one lucky person.

Spiced chai

Chai is delicious hot or iced, but the premixed stuff available at the supermarket is so expensive. Do as the rest of the world does and make your own!

Get it:

2 cups milk
2 cups water
4 teaspoons black tea leaves
   or 4 bags of black tea

1 tablespoon spice mix (see below)
1–2 tablespoons sugar, to taste

Chai spice mix:
1 tablespoon ground
   cardamom pods
1 tablespoon cinnamon
2 teaspoons ground ginger

2 teaspoons whole cloves
2 teaspoons whole coriander
   seeds
1 teaspoon black peppercorns

(You can find ground spices in bulk at most natural food stores, or give your coffee grinder a good cleaning and grind your own.)

Make it: Blend all chai spice mix ingredients together. Store in a dark, airtight container.

Combine milk and water in a saucepan and bring to a boil over medium heat, stirring constantly. Reduce heat to low, add the loose tea or tea bags, and add well-shaken spice mix to taste. Remove from heat, cover, and steep for five minutes. Strain into a mug and add sugar to taste. Makes one serving. Note: Use vanilla soy milk for a creamy soy chai!

Juicy sun tea

Sun tea is a summer classic. All you need is a clear glass container with a good lid, a sunny back porch or windowsill, a few hours, and the following ingredients. (This particular recipe is my favorite because it's juicy and sweet!)

Get it:

³/₄ cup black tea leaves
or 10 black tea bags
6 cups cold water
4 tablespoons sugar

1 sprig fresh mint
2 cups fresh orange, raspberry,
or apple juice
3 tablespoons fresh lemon juice

Make it: Put the tea, water, sugar, and mint into a clear glass container, screw on the lid, shake, and place in the piping-hot sun for at least three hours. Strain into a pitcher, add the juices, stir, and chill. For extra-fancy flair, garnish with fresh mint, orange slices, raspberries, or apple wedges. Makes 2 servings.

Green chai margarita

The traditional tea geishas of Japan might be shocked to hear of such an uncivilized concoction, but as far as I'm concerned, the green chai margarita is the only way to properly take tea on a hot, summer afternoon. Makes one serving.

Get it:

2½ tablespoons tequila
1 tablespoon fresh lemon juice
2 tablespoons Cointreau
2 tablespoons sugar

10 green chai ice cubes
(see below)
1 lime wedge

Make it (well in advance):

Green chai ice cubes:

1 teaspoon ground cinnamon
1 teaspoon whole cloves
1 teaspoon whole coriander
seeds
1 teaspoon black peppercorns

1½ tablespoons ground
cardamom pods
Pinch of anise seeds
1 cup sencha green tea leaves

Stir all ingredients together in a medium-sized bowl until very well mixed and steep for five minutes or to taste (1 tablespoon of mix per 1 cup hot water). Pour into an ice cube tray, and freeze.

Margarita: Combine tequila, lemon juice, Cointreau, sugar, and chai cubes in a blender until perfectly slushy. Add more sugar to taste. Pour in a sugar-rimmed glass and garnish with a fresh lime wedge. Makes one serving.

Bubble tea fever!

Bubble tea is the teenage rage in Asia, and the fever is quickly spreading west. Bubble tea is black or green tea mixed with a flavored syrup or powder, then served in a glass with big, gooey tapioca pearls ("bubbles") floating on the bottom. The syrups come in yummy flavors like taro, honeydew, and coconut. Go to www.bubbleteasupply.com for the inside dish on bubble tea.

The Hostess with the Mostess

. . . .

The single most important factor in determining the success of any private gathering is not the music, the wine, nor the food—it's you. As the hostess, you have the power to make or break any game night, dinner party, or secret club meeting. If you're relaxed and having a good time, your guests will be relaxed and have a good time; but if you're uptight or unsure of yourself, your guests will squirm in their seats. The secret weapon of all successful hostesses is confidence. You want your guests to feel at ease, so you must blaze the path of nonchalance, even if you have to fake it. Who cares if you burned the Chex mix, don't have enough chairs, and your chihuahua peed on the floor? Brush it off. Or better yet, turn up the music and dance it off. If you can roll with the party punches and laugh at yourself, your friends will laugh along with you (and maybe a little bit at you, but they are your friends). Here are a few easy-to-follow tips to help your Saturday night soirees or Scrabble nights forever be fabulous. Remember, even if you're just having a couple of the girls over for sangria and *Some Like It Hot*, it's all in the details. Go the extra mile to make it special and unexpected, and by the end of the evening, you will be the hostess with the mostess.

Invitations: Everybody loves getting invitations, especially if it's to a casual get-together between friends. Make your own invites by scanning and printing out funny photos of your friends, folding origami invites, or cutting out pictures from old magazines. If you're in a time pinch, go to the drugstore and buy some Barbie or Powerpuff Girls invites, so fancy! Be specific on the day, time, and if your friends should bring anything. RSVP? Definitely. You need to know how many pillows to fluff or card tables to set out.

🎵 **Themes:** Whether you're having a hard-core poker night or just some close friends over for tea, giving your party a theme can really spice things up. Some of my favorites are: best of the '80s, prom night, trailer park, Viva Las Vegas, or the off-season holiday (New Year's in August).

🍸 **Eats and drinks:** You can ask friends to bring a bottle of wine or bag of chips, but a good hostess always feeds her guests. Keep it simple: veggies and dip, bread and cheese, olives; if you're in a pinch, visit a gourmet food store and pick up some already prepared goodies. If your gathering has a purpose, let your food play along. Your green-chai margarita party (see page 137) might offer plates of ceviche and sashimi; your book club review of *Like Water for Chocolate* might feature a gooey chocolate fondue!

 Space: It doesn't matter how much space you have, it's all about what you do with it. Keep furniture, and people, together. Don't set your sofa and chairs against the walls so that people stare across the room at each other. Make the arrangement cozy and intimate, with extra pillows. Make sure people have a place to put their drinks and plates, and break out the coasters for wood tables. Place a piece of lovely fabric over your television screen (unless it's movie night)—it's funny how people will stare at the screen even when it's off.

Vibe: The two most important elements in setting a party's vibe are the lighting and the music. The ambient light of candles and floor and table lamps creates a warm, inviting atmosphere. Of course, bright light is necessary if you plan on playing cards or a board game, but keep it localized. Place a bright lamp near the activity area, and keep the rest of your nest bathed in softer light. Choose music to set the mood. A Japanese tea party calls for Cibo Matto; keep a mojito party real with the Cuban flavor of Celia Cruz; for a wine-tasting party, lounge music from Julie London fits the bill.

Party favors: Disposable cameras for all to use, Silly String, streamers, plastic decoder rings—nothing peps up a party faster than favors. And don't let anyone leave without receiving something to remember the gathering by, like their very own goodie bag. Fill it with dice or a deck of foxy picture cards for game night, jasmine tea or bath salts for group spa day, a glue stick and stickers for a scrapbooking club—you get the idea. You can also throw in little plastic toys, party Polaroids, a mixed CD—then top it off with a personal thank-you note. Now that's how to play the perfect hostess!

Games Galore

Card games

In the past, cards have been banned, burned, and even called devil's work. Fewer than a hundred years ago, any lady who played cards for money was herself considered a wild card! Thankfully, card playing managed to survive the ages, and today's lady-run bridge clubs and poker nights are a respectable dime a dozen. So why is card playing so addictive? Because it's competitive but social, stimulating but meditative; and being part of a regular game is a great way to get friends together and relax, laugh, catch up, and outsmart each other. Why not hostess a card night at your place? Here's a breakdown of the most popular fifty-two-card favorites for two or more. To learn how to play them, and others like the down-and-dirty Oh Hell, the Jamaican Super Kalooki, and the Chinese Zhen Fen, check out www.pagat.com.

Card game fab 5

Bridge: Played in kitchens, clubs, and tournaments throughout the world, bridge is complex and complicated, but that's the allure. With a little patience, anyone can learn to play, and you can always improve. Played with one deck of cards and four players divided into two partnerships.

Poker: Poker is so popular it's been called the national card game of the United States. There are more forms of poker than you can throw a chip at: the standard five-card stud, Mexican stud, draw, lowball, even strip; and they almost always involve one deck of cards, one fifth of whisky, and two or more people bluffing about holding flushes, straights, and full houses.

Basic rummy: Developed in the smoky saloons of the late nineteenth century, rummy is a snap to learn and offers plenty of opportunity to squash an opponent. One deck of cards is played as two to six players try to dispose of all their cards by melding them into groups of the same number, or numerical sequences of the same suit. In the simpler version of gin rummy, only two people can play, but you can always play two or more separate games simultaneously.

Canasta: Canasta is like rummy on steroids. Originally from Uruguay, canasta is played with two decks of cards and four players divided into two partnerships. Like rummy, the players meld the cards together into groups, but throw a few canastas (a meld of seven cards) in there, and the game heats up until one of the partnerships scores a whopping 5,000 points.

Hearts: A card game with cult status, hearts is one of the few games where you try not to accumulate points. The game revolves around taking tricks (piles of played cards), and every seasoned hearts player knows to avoid all cards in the hearts suit, high cards, and most of all, the evil queen of spades. One deck of cards and three to seven people can play all night long.

Hearts & diamonds

The fifty-two-card deck we use today is a direct descendant of cards used in thirteenth-century France. The French cards contained four suits of thirteen cards each, and each suit represented a class of French society. Hearts represented the church, spades the army, diamonds the merchants, and clubs the peasants and farmers.

Group games

Sometimes you feel like putting the deck away and just letting loose—it's time to break out those group games! With minimal preparation, you can throw together a beach blanket bingo party, an exotic sake and mah-jongg party, or a flirtatious night of co-ed twister. The sky's the limit; just get your nest ready for a night full of laughs and more than a few memorable moments. As some people are hesitant to get involved in group games, here are a few of the more enticing ones to help lure your friends over—a couple bottles of bubbly doesn't hurt either!

Bingo: In order to throw a bona fide bingo night, dress up your nest like a high school gym or tacky church activity room and keep the spiked punch flowing. Or put down the beach blankets, break out the bikinis, blow up the beach balls, and crank up the heat for a rockin' beach bingo party!

Mah-jongg: Raise the red lanterns, listen to a Chinese opera on CD, and order takeout. Mah-jongg is a Chinese game played with tiles that have pretty dragon and flower images on them. Your guests are sure to be captivated by the exotic beauty and cutthroat savageness of the game. Best played with four players, but can be played with three.

Charades: Charades can be played totally spur of the moment. No boards, dice, or cards necessary—just a few friends, two teams, and a bit of wine. Charades is always a blast because even your most shy and buttoned-up of friends will suddenly be imitating Lucille Ball or acting out a scene from a kung fu film.

Trivial Pursuit: What better way to get your intellectual, science geek, and pop princess pals together in one room for a night of strong cocktails, light academics, and surly social amusement? Two to six players can play, and breaking into teams makes it much more interesting.

Oldies but goodies

Sometimes the best games are the classics—the ones that we've played at countless family nights, birthday parties, and sleepovers.

Why? They remind us of a simpler time, when the mere sight of the Candyland board made our mouths water, and the only paycheck we had to sweat for was the passing of Go in Monopoly. Plus, everybody already knows how to play the classics, so everyone can jump right in. The oldies are such good old-fashioned fun, why not throw a retro game night? Dust off your old Mystery Date, break out the Kool-Aid, and rent the original episodes of *The Brady Bunch* on DVD. Tell your friends to bring their favorite classic so you'll have plenty to go around. Heck, why not just tell your friends to bring their sleeping bags as well and make it a slumber party? It's like being ten again, minus the bra freezing and retainers.

Top 10 classic games

* Battleship   * Scrabble
* Clue   * Sorry
* The Game of Life   * Trouble
* Monopoly   * Twister
* Risk   * Yahtzee

You can buy all of these games at toy stores or at www .boardgames.com, but some have been upgraded with plastic and electronic devices. If you want the real deal, look at thrift stores or on eBay.

The Gang's All Here

· ·

You don't always need a deck of cards or board games to get the gang together and share the love. It's all about having a good time in your nest, right? So take charge and come up with your own activity! Get a Stich 'n Bitch going. Does the gang drool over the sandy-blond locks of Brad Pitt? Pop the corn, pour the Pepsi, run to the video store, and have a Brad-athon! Believe me, you won't have to wrack your brain too long before you hit upon a golden activity to share with your friends. Remember—the reason is always really just an excuse.

Group spa day

Break out the facial masks, nail polish, and foot baths and invite the girls over for an afternoon of pampering, polishing, and preening! No one can resist a group spa day, but before your friends arrive, take an hour and get your nest ready for an afternoon of sinful self-indulgence. Here are some ideas on how to turn your nest into your very own chez spa; but remember, ask your friends to bring their favorite beauty goodies so you won't have to fork out the dough for an industrial-size bottle of nail polish remover. Oh, and put the word out that the party's BYOR (bring your own robe!).

Plan the services: Unless you want people hopping in and out of your shower, it's best to keep things like body scrubs and wraps off the agenda; there are plenty of less messy treatments to choose from. Set up a manicure table stocked with soaking bowls, polishes, remover, files, and cuticle scissors; and a steam-facial table where people can fill bowls with hot water, add a couple drops of essential oil, put a towel over their head, and sweat it out. Stock your kitchen counter with scrumptious-looking face masks—take them out of their containers and put them into bowls on ice, like a salad bar. So Euro! Set up a pedicure chair with a foot-soaking tub and plenty of magazines. If you really want your place to feel like a spa, ask your friends to pamper one another in shifts. Maybe set up a give-one, get-one policy—give a manicure, then get a facial!

Plan the space: Make sure you have enough "work space" and "equipment." You'll want at least one manicure table that doesn't wobble, and a comfy pedicure chair. Put pillows on the floor so your friends can sit, lounge, and lay down if they wish. Make sure you have tons of magazines, the trashier the better. You'll also need plenty of washcloths, hand towels, and ponytail holders. Put a couple of tea kettles or large pans on the stove for heating water for steam facials, foot baths, face washes, and tea.

Create the ambience: Burn a light, natural incense, or better yet, essential oils in an oil burner (see page 54). Turn down the overhead lights and light some candles. Put on some music that takes you away, like Saint Etienne, Café del Mar, or any meditative, ambient music.

Make the goods: While you've asked everyone to bring their favorite beauty products, you are the hostess, so you should have a smorgasbord of spa stuff on hand. Sound expensive? It doesn't have to be. See Make It a Spa Day on page 52 for a bevy of DIY beauty recipes, most of which can be made in under thirty minutes.

Snacks

Preening, magazine reading, and gossiping all day works up quite an appetite! Refreshments are definitely called for, but keep them light and healthy. Make sure the herbal tea and mineral water with lemon flow freely. Fresh fruit and vegetables are great to nibble on while your facial mask is drying; bread and cheese is a more substantial snack if you're reading the fall fashion issue of *Vogue*. If you really want to make your spa day a hit, put a little chocolate on the table. It doesn't matter if it's hot cocoa, Nutella, M&M's, or Ghirardelli bars; chocolate is always the ultimate indulgence and the perfect complement to your chez spa.

Stitch 'n Bitch it

Stitch 'n Bitches, or weekly knitting sessions, were first held by disgruntled housewives in the 1950s who used to get together and air their domestic frustrations while knitting and doing other needle crafts. Today the members come from all walks of life, from hipsters to single moms, from corporate execs to grannies; but it's still as much about dishing your love life as it is sharing knitting tips. The modern Stitch 'n Bitch is a highly respected institution within the knitting community, and weekly groups have been founded across the country from Portland, Oregon, to New York City. How about hostessing a Stich 'n Bitch at your place? Put the idea out to your fellow knitters. If you can't get enough knitters together from your regular group of friends, put up signs at your local yarn stores—and make new ones! If you call, they will come. In the meantime, here are a few pointers to get you started.

The secret to Stitch 'n Bitch success: Set a day and time, and make it official. Get crafty and send out homemade announcements with pieces of yarn or kitsch knitting images on them. Once the word's out, get your nest ready for knitting. Make sure you have plenty of seats, pillows, and music. Ask your members to help bring the food, and give the gathering a theme like margaritas and Mexican, beer and pizza, or mimosas and Belgian waffles. For more information on the world of organized knitting (and images for your announcements), go to www.stitchnbitch.org.

Book clubs

Book clubs, or literary societies, as they used to be called, are so much more than just a bunch of people getting together to discuss a book. They are a forum for discussion of all kinds of issues: literary, social, political, racial. Books are just a reflection of life, right? So are the discussions at book club meetings. They offer an opportunity to talk and listen, and a place for your ideas on everything from feminism to face-lifts. Is your interest piqued? Maybe you should start a book club of your own. But do keep in mind, the best book clubs are the ones that have members with differing opinions and views. Try to get a group of friends together from different walks of life, from prom queens to indie girls, soccer moms to starving artists—the opposing opinions will make your discussions all the more interesting. Here's a few more things to keep in mind when starting a book club.

* There are two basic types of clubs: clubs that read everything under the sun, from Edith Wharton to Jackie Collins, and clubs that read only nonfiction, or subversive feminist lit, or Oprah's picks. Think about what you like to read, and decide if you want your club to be open book or have a specific focus.

* You'll need to assign a leader, a person in charge of driving the discussion. This person should really read the book, research the time period, the author—even if it means buying the CliffsNotes! Rotating leaders is always a good idea, as it keeps any one person from dominating the group. It gives shy bookworms an opportunity to break out of their shells, and just keeps things fresh.

* Unless your members are hard-core readers, meeting any more than once a month may be too much, unless you're reading Harlequins!

* A cocktail or two may loosen tongues, but this is no place for a full bar. Alcohol kills intellect and fans emotions, a sloppy combination for any meeting of the minds.

* A club meeting doesn't have to mean just sitting in someone's living room. Play a game of croquet in the park after reading *Remains of the Day*; sip sake and discuss *Memoirs of a Geisha*; or better yet, read this book and then throw a crafts night!

Potluck it

Every club meeting, get-together, and party is better with food, and as the hostess, it's up to you to make sure there's plenty to go around. What? You don't cook save for toast and reheating takeout? No problem. Make your get-together a potluck. Choose a theme like Mexican, Indian, comfort food, or summer picnic, and ask each of your friends to bring a specific dish, like an appetizer, salad, entree, or dessert. Less work for you, more good food for everyone!

Movie marathons

It's Friday night and everybody's pooped after working all week. What to do? Pop the corn, turn off the lights, and have the gang over to your place for a movie night! Movie nights are deliciously low on energy, easy on the nest, and a cinch to throw together at the last minute. But keep it interesting. Instead of going to Blockbuster and swimming in the new releases aisle, shake up the menu by renting something unexpected, old, or quirky. Rent a classic, a foreign film, a cult film, or a blast from your past. In case you're the type of person who can name a dozen must-see movies off the top of your head, but once you step into the video store your mind goes blank, here's a list of some all-time fabulous flicks. Write a few of them down before you go DVD hunting next time.

Best coiffs: *Dogtown and Z-Boys, Hairspray, Heavy Metal Parking Lot, Party Monster, Saturday Night Fever, Shampoo*

Best lines: *Fast Times at Ridgemont High, Ferris Bueller's Day Off, Heathers, Napoleon Dynamite, This Is Spinal Tap, Welcome to the Dollhouse*

Best threads: *Barbarella, Boogie Nights, Kill Bill, Pretty in Pink, Purple Rain, Strictly Ballroom*

Chick flicks: *Fried Green Tomatoes, How Stella Got Her Groove Back, Laurel Canyon, Mystic Pizza, Terminator 2: Judgment Day, Thelma & Louise, Woman of the Year*

Comedies: *Best in Show, Earth Girls Are Easy, Foul Play, Meet the Parents, Monty Python and the Holy Grail, 200 Cigarettes, The Wedding Singer*

Foreign films: *Amélie, City of God, La Dolce Vita, La Femme Nikita, Life Is Beautiful, Whale Rider*

Hunk alerts: any Sean Connery James Bond movie, *The English Patient, Legends of the Fall, The Pianist, Raiders of the Lost Ark, Top Gun*

Movies that make you go hmm . . . : *Bowling for Columbine, The Endless Summer, The Eyes of Tammy Faye, Microcosmos, Spellbound, SuperSize Me*

Musicals: *Chicago, Grease, Moulin Rouge!, The Sound of Music, West Side Story, Willie Wonka & the Chocolate Factory, Xanadu*

Scary movies: *Carrie, The Exorcist, Glitter, Halloween, Nightmare on Elm Street, Psycho, The Shining*

Sci-fi: *Alien, Blade Runner, eXistenZ, Planet of the Apes, Star Wars, 2001: A Space Odyssey*

Swoony classics: *Bridget Jones's Diary, Casablanca, Dangerous Liasons, Out of Africa, Roman Holiday, Say Anything*

Tearjerkers: *Bambi, The Color Purple, E.T., Love Story, Rabbit-Proof Fence, Terms of Endearment*

You're invited to a slumber party!

Whatever happened to the slumber party? Once a coveted, all-night girl-fest filled with dancing and sugar and truth or dares, the slumber party seemingly disappeared along with braces and training bras. What a shame. As a misguided youth, the slumber party may have seemed like a night of freedom away from the parents, but in reality it was, and always will be, a night of female bonding. Proof of my point: Remember how after a slumber party, you'd go to school the next Monday and feel that your relationships with the girls present had somehow shifted—like you all shared the same secret? That's the power of the slumber party. It brings girls together, and that's a darn good reason to revive this fun, feminist tradition. Send out invites and ask your friends to bring snacks, games, and of course, their sleeping bags. Play truth or dare, or Mystery Date, or strip poker. Pull a Pink Lady and talk about boys all night in your lingerie; or just lounge around in flannel watching Audrey Hepburn movies while snuggled in your sleeping bags. Get silly; get philosophical; get amped on Red Bulls; get sleepy on Couvoisier—whatever you do, just hang out with your girlfriends, all night long. Since you're all adults now and your parents won't be picking you up the next morning, top off your night of bonding by going out to breakfast together the next morning!

Clothing swaps

A clothing swap is like a garage sale, except it's just you and your friends and everything's free. The idea is for a bunch of friends to bring over a box or two of clothes they don't want anymore, and then everyone haggles and begs and fights for the choice pieces. Clothing swaps are usually based on the bartering system, like "I'll trade you those Calvins for this Lacoste," but you can buy or sell clothes for favors, too. Car washings, home-baked chocolate chip cookies, and dog sitting are always valuable trading chips. Just invite all your gals and fashion-conscious guys over for an afternoon or evening of ohhing, ahhing, grabbing, and swapping. It's a great way to get everybody together, score a bunch of fancy new clothes on the cheap, and clean out your closet to boot!

Nesting party

Addicted to *Trading Spaces* and *Queer Eye for the Straight Guy*? Can't wait to try some of the home improvements and crafts listed in this book? If you've always secretly wanted to be Katie Brown, now's your chance. Ring up your fellow domestic divas and have them over for a nesting party hosted by you! Designate specific topics or crafts; they could be as simple as colorwashing or as involved as hardwood-floor refinishing, and tell your friends to come prepared to discuss and maybe even demonstrate. Share your herb garden success stories; dish about painting techniques, window coverings, or sewing. Or get crafty with it—have everyone chip in for ingredients to make facial scrubs and body packs, or soap and candles. How very nesty of you! But beyond the fun and cleverness, perhaps the biggest perk of hostessing a nesting party is that you and your friends can work together to make your nests more comfortable, more chic, and more you. I truly hope that this book will help inspire all of you in that endeavor.

Happy nesting!

Thank You

Kudos to the following books for their pertinent information and ongoing inspiration:

Aromatherapy Handbook for Beauty, Hair, and Skin Care, Erich Keller
The Book of Green Tea, Diana Rosen
Clean House, Clean Planet, Karen Logan
Clean, Naturally, Sandy Maine
The Good Earth Bath, Beauty & Health Book, Casey Kellar
Herbs, Greens & Aromatics, Millie Owen
How to Grow Fresh Air, Dr. B. C. Wolverton
The Natural Paint Book, Lynn Edwards and Julia Lawless
The New Tea Book, Sara Perry
Stitch 'n Bitch, Debbie Stoller
Successful Houseplants, Andrew Clinch
Super Suite, Mark Montano
The Ultimate Scrapbooking Book, Rebecca Carter, Vanessa-Ann, Sandi Genovese, Lael C. Furgeson, Stephanie F. Taylor

About the Author

Michelle Kehm attended the School of Journalism at the University of Oregon. She has written for *The New York Times, SELF, BUST,* and chickclick.com. and her travel stories have been published in the anthologies *The Unsavvy Traveler* and *A Woman Alone*. She divides her time between Portland, Oregon, and New York City.

Notes